Jewish Wisdom
for
Living *and* Dying

JEWISH WISDOM
for
LIVING *and* DYING

A Spiritual Journey Through the Prayers
and Rituals of *Maavor Yabok*
and *Sefer HaHayiim*

Steven Moss

Foreword by Simcha Paull Raphael

RESOURCE *Publications* · Eugene, Oregon

JEWISH WISDOM FOR LIVING AND DYING
A Spiritual Journey Through the Prayers and Rituals of *Maavor Yabok*
and *Sefer HaHayiim*

Resource Publications
An Imprint of Wipf and Stock Publishers
199 W. 8th Ave., Suite 3
Eugene, OR 97401

www.wipfandstock.com

PAPERBACK ISBN: 978-1-6667-5039-3
HARDCOVER ISBN: 978-1-6667-5040-9
EBOOK ISBN: 978-1-6667-5041-6

AUGUST 15, 2022 1:06 PM

I composed new ideas and different explanations . . . to offer them as an offering and as incense in love and in reverence before the holy congregations, in order that it will make a way in the midst of the shaking worlds, . . . a bridge from the world of change and destruction with its sinful heavenly condition to be joined with the pleasures of Unity, Blessing, and Holiness

RABBI AARON BERECHIAH, MODENA,
MAAVOR YABOK

And therefore, I called the book of the law of kindness and truth, *Sefer HaHayiim*, that by it he will be worthy of being written in the book of life and will have the fear of heaven

SIMON FRANKFURTER, AMSTERDAM,
SEFER HAHAYIIM

Contents

Foreword

According to Rabbi Moses Isserles "*One who visited a sick person and did not offer a prayer on their behalf, has not fulfilled the mitzvah of bikkur cholim, visiting the sick.*" *(Yoreh Deah, 335, 4)*
I recall being sixteen years old and walking into the hospital room to visit my grandfather after he had a heart attack. Nothing in my life had prepared me for what I encountered—a complex array of medical technology, tubes, wires, and flashing lights all connected to my beloved grandfather, seemingly keeping him alive. I was traumatized by that experience, and in reflecting upon it over fifty years later, I felt totally helpless to do anything to offer my Zaydi any kind of caring, compassion or support. I smiled at him through the mask of medical machinery covering his face and probably slipped out of the room as quickly as possible in total discomfort.

I don't remember anyone else being in the room at the time, and I certainly have no recollections of any healing prayers; and there was nothing particularly Jewish about that encounter. Yet my grandfather was quintessentially an "old world Jew", a simple man who worked his entire adult life in a garment factory in the city of Montreal. Born in Eastern Europe, he emigrated to Canada as a young man, and though Yiddish was his first language, prided himself on speaking English without an accent. Throughout his life the rubrics of Judaism were central to who he was, to what he did. No one would have ever described him as an assimilated Jew. He and my grandmother had a kosher home, observed Shabbat and all the Jewish holy days, even if not traditional or Orthodox in practice. Nonetheless, we celebrated Passover Seders in my grand-parents' home, on Yom Kippur my grandfather always fasted, and since he had sung in a High Holy Day choir in his younger years, would tell the tale of his frequent long treks across the city to arrive at synagogue punctually for Rosh HaShanah and Yom Kippur services.

And yet, in that time of crisis and sickness after his heart attack, what were the Jewish resources present for him as he lay in a hospital bed close to death? As far as I could tell, there was very little Jewish spiritual support available for him, nor for other members of our family. In that era rabbis were not being trained in pastoral care; there were no books available in English on Jewish care for the sick and dying; and our family knew nothing about a *bikkur cholim* society for visiting the sick. Most likely the only chaplain affiliated with the hospital was a Catholic priest who performed last rites for dying Catholic patients. And Jewish rituals and prayers for the sick and dying? Certainly not.

My grandfather and I were not the only ones without a spiritual and functional framework to meet the needs of the moment when faced with sickness and death. This dearth of efficacious Jewish deathbed traditions impacted an entire generation of Jews.

There is another story along these lines told about an eight-five year old Jewish woman, dying in Brooklyn Convalescent Hospital. Her daughter, a well-intentioned baby-boomer, wanted to go read her mother passages from *Bardo Thodol*, the Tibetan Book of Dead. This sixteenth-century Buddhist deathbed manual composed in the monasteries of ancient Tibet depicts visions of dancing Dakini goddesses and flaming wrathful Heruka Buddhas one encounters upon leaving the body. Stephen Levine, an early pioneer doing spiritual work with the dying, warned the woman that reading that text would likely scare and confuse her poor mother. "Go read her old Yiddish love poetry," he advised. But again, where were the available Jewish resources? There are books of the dead all around the world. We have heard of the Tibetan Book of Dead, the Egyptian Book of the Dead, certainly Christianity has deathbed rituals and prayers coming out the medieval tradition of *Ars Moriendi*, the art of dying. And more recently we have been introduced to books of the dead, or prayer traditions for accompanying the dying from various indigenous cultures. And the Jewish Book of the Dead?

It turns out, as Steven Moss articulates in *Jewish Wisdom for Living and Dying: A Spiritual Journey through Prayers and Rituals of* Maavor Yabok *and* Sefer HaHayyim, Judaism does have a very extensive legacy of teachings and sacred texts on dealing with sickness, dying, death and the afterlife. Dating back to the post-Talmudic tractate *Semahot*, on practices of death and mourning, and continuing through the medieval era and into modernity, Judaism produced scores of texts on death, dying and post-mortem survival, most of which have been totally lost to our contemporary Jewish world. Over the course of the 20th century—especially after World War II and the Holocaust—scientific rationalism, secularization of religion and a cultural discomfort talking about death stripped away interest in anything having to do with prayer traditions for the sick and dying. Furthermore, as a result of migrations of Jews from the traditional Jewish cultures of Eastern Europe and Mediterranean lands to North America, Jewish wisdom on sickness, death, and dying slipped out of view, vanquished into the dustbin of history, or, at best, into arcane libraries of academic Jewish learning.

As he tells the story, as a young rabbinical student and a novice chaplain, Steven Moss heard the call to explore the text that can most closely be understood to be a Jewish Book of the Dead, *Maavor Yabok*, the central manual of the Jewish burial societies of Southern, Central and Eastern Europe for centuries. That sacred text, as well as *Sefer HaHayyim*, a collection of prayers for the sick and dying from late 18th century Amsterdam, literally called out to our author to bring their contents out of the library stacks into the hands of those caring for the sick and dying today.

Over forty years ago, I had the opportunity to read Rabbi Moss's Rabbinic thesis. At the time, as I was beginning my own work studying Jewish views of the afterlife, I felt that book needed to be published one day. As life teaches us all, everything happens in its own time, its own rhythm. As we have seen, COVID-19 has catalyzed a shifting of priorities bringing health care and illness more sharply into focus. In ways we might not have predicted, the time has arrived.

In this pandemic era of death and loss caused by a stealth virus, circumstances are now ripe for Steven Moss's extensive research and scholarly writings to see the light of day. Four decades later we finally get to read the act of literary archeology he has accomplished. In translating, interpreting and delineating the prayer traditions of *Maavor Yabok* and *Sefer HaHayyim*, this book brings the legacy of Jewish deathbed traditions into the 21st century. Through this unique book we are invited to explore a wide assortment and literary pastiche of Jewish prayers and rituals for the end-of-life journey. And while these prayers are not written in the metaphors and language of contemporary life, the passion and profundity of these age-old prayers invite us to imagine being present with others who are dealing with life-threatening illness, or preparing to leave this world behind. *Jewish Wisdom for Living and Dying: A Spiritual Journey through Prayers and Rituals of* Maavor Yabok *and* Sefer HaHayyim invites each of us to think deeply about the efficacy of prayers for the sick and dying in our own times, and what prayers for healing mean to each of us individually.

It is more than fifty years since the pioneering work of the Swiss psychiatrist Dr. Elizabeth Kübler-Ross spawned a cultural transformation of attitudes towards dying and death. Today, we are engaged in bringing back to life long-lost Jewish traditions on dying, death and afterlife. At the same time, we are witnessing the emergence and proliferation of important and sophisticated revolutionary trends in care for the dying and bereaved. The continual spread of the hospice movement; training of a growing cadre of death doulas; international expansion of legalized medical aid in dying; future use of psychedelics with terminal patients; growth of green burial and home funeral practices; resurgence of Chevra Kaddisha practices in both traditional and liberal Jewish communities; the Death Café movement; and so many other innovations are all part of the burgeoning of expanded and transformed attitudes and practices of dying and death. Clearly a widespread revolution in death care is happening in our times.

Against this background, *Jewish Wisdom for Living and Dying: A Spiritual Journey through Prayers and Rituals of* Maavor Yabok *and* Sefer HaHayyim is a wonderful contribution to the emerging Jewish literature on death and dying. Undoubtedly, this is a book that can be read cover to cover. At the same time, this is book to be studied like a *sefer,* a traditional sacred Hebrew text that can be savored and returned to over and over. Each page, each painstaking translation can be studied for its depth and wisdom as a doorway into the mysterious and complex world of the end-of-life journey. This book is a gift from the past to the evolving future of death care. We are grateful to Steven Moss for his persistent and courageous work bringing the legacy of this lost wisdom to our attention.

Stephen Levine, *Who Dies? An Investigation of Conscious Living and Conscious Dying* (Garden City, NY: Anchor Books, 1982), p. 272

Simcha Paull Raphael, Ph.D.
DA'AT Institute for Death Awareness, Advocacy and Training

ACKNOWLEDGMENTS

I RECOGNIZE THE PAST lives who have played such an important part in my spiritual journey. I am grateful to my grandmother's grandfather Rabbi Zev Wolf Turbowitz, Av Bet Din, Kraziai, Lithuania. I carry his soul in mine, and his influence in my life is greater than he ever could have imagined. I thank Rabbi Aaron Berechiah of Modena who, since my rabbinic school days, has pursued me to work on his incredible text, *Maavor Yabok*. Finally, I shall always be grateful to my parents, Doris, and Ira, who taught me how to appreciate education and life.

There are not enough words in any language to express my thanks to the love of my life, my wife Judy. Not only did she encourage me in my studies in rabbinic school, but she continues to support me in the work that I do now.

An additional thank you to my editors and proofreaders, Gerri Burgert, Rick Light, and Reb Simcha Raphael. Their keen eyes to find errors of all sorts were invaluable.

Note: Unless noted otherwise, all translations from the Hebrew of *Maavor Yabok* are my own. Unless within a quotation from a book, all biblical translations are my own.

To the Reader

Essentially, this book is a manifesto for the need to write a *Maavor Yabok* for the 21st century. As such, this book is written particularly for members of *Chevra Kadisha*, holy burial societies in the Jewish community. It is my hope that individuals who are looking to the Jewish sources for comfort and strength, as he or she faces illness or dying, will also find this book helpful. I also hope it will be of benefit to individuals who are simply interested in this literature, and the time and place in which they were written.

Chapter I

AN INTRODUCTION TO THE TWO BOOKS

BOOKS HAVE A WAY of calling out to me! This journey with a book entitled *Maavor Yabok* began as I was walking through the stacks of the library of Hebrew Union College–Jewish Institute of Religion (HUC-JIR), the rabbinical school in New York where I received my ordination. I was looking through the books in the section on rituals and prayers for the sick and dying. At the time, I was serving as chaplain and consultant at various hospitals and hospice programs in New York, and I wanted to know what assistance the Jewish sources could give me in this work. I was also looking for books that could help me in writing my ordination thesis, which was also on the topic of caring for the sick and the dying.

There were, of course, many books on the shelves in this section and in this area of my interest, since this was a professional school that prepared its students for the rabbinate and congregational life. As I walked along the shelves, one book seduced me that day. It called out to me, "Take me. I am the book you want!" The book was *Maavor Yabok*, first published in 1626 by Rabbi Aaron Berechiah of Modena, Italy. What impressed me most about this book were the number of editions of the book on the shelves. This told me it must be an important work. It turned out to be particularly important for me because, not only did it become the basis for my thesis, but many decades later, I am still working on my translation of the text, and I am still sharing its teachings in various settings.

One purpose of this book, *Jewish Wisdom for Living and Dying*, is to share my thesis, that I originally wrote in 1974 in a more accessible and user-friendly form. The thesis analyzed the sections in two books, *Maavor Yabok* and *Sefer HaHayiim*, that focused on prayers and rituals used by a person when sick and or dying. Although both books were equally important at the time and place of their publications, the influence of *Maavor Yabok* was greater, as shown by its more than twenty printed editions, including modern editions, and the publication of various *Maavor Yabok* manuals. I was also more interested in *Maavor Yabok* because of the details used by Berechiah to describe the Kabbalistic meanings and functions to all the prayers, rituals, and beliefs. I was a student of Kabbalah and fascinated to see how Berechiah applied its teachings to these acts of kindness as well as the work of the *Chevra Kadisha*.

Regarding my thesis, I wanted to compare these two works to see how they differed in their presentation of this material, whether they were influenced by the time and place in which they were written, as well as the differences in the books' authors. *Jewish Wisdom For Living and Dying*, expresses my interest in studying and analyzing these texts for both the rituals and the meanings behind the rituals that could be used today by members of a *Chevra Kadisha*, a dedicated group of men and women trained in the rituals and prayers of caring for the sick, the dying, and the dead.

My intention is that this book will be useful to *Chevra Kadisha* members, individuals experiencing illness, facing one's death, and/or looking for direction and help from the Jewish tradition. It, hopefully, will also be valuable to those caring for people going through these difficult life experiences.

The most complete and detailed study of these handbooks and the communal groups from which they arose is the work *Communal Sick-Care in the German Ghetto*, by Jacob P. Marcus. He determines that these and other liturgical collections for the sick and dying were the products of "Holy Brotherhoods," called in Hebrew *Chevra Kadisha*. These brotherhoods developed amid the historical and sociological turmoil of the Middle Ages, beginning primarily in the late 16th century. These brotherhoods, however, did not become fully developed structures until their appearance in Italy. This was where *Maavor Yabok* was written.

As Marcus describes the early developments of this movement:

> The Spanish expulsions brought about another trend which undoubtedly played a part in stimulating the creations of Brotherhoods in Italy. During the same century, the sixteenth, that Spanish Jews brought the confraternity idea to Italy, others were developing a cabbalistic school of thought in Palestine, a school of thought which laid great emphasis on the spiritual meaning of death, and on the protection of the soul before and after departure from the body. This concentration on the spiritual care of the dying and of the dead expressed itself in special liturgies for the deathbed which were developed in classical form during the period 1615–1710.[1]

The earliest of these manuals was *Maaneh Lashon*, which was printed in 1615. By 1800, it had gone through some forty editions. It is not included for discussion here because it primarily concentrated on prayers for the dead, and less on prayers for the sick and the dying. *Maavor Yabok* and *Sefer HaHayiim*, however, discuss all of these areas of life, dying, and death.

On the popularity of *Maavor Yabok* and *Sefer HaHayiim*, Marcus writes:

> Only two editions of this work appeared before 1800, but at least eighteen editions in abbreviated form—*Kizzur Maabar Yabbok*—appeared from 1682 to 1800. . . . The *Kizzur Maabar Yabbok* was the standard liturgical work of its type, and was widely used, not only in Italy, but throughout the German lands where it appeared under a variety of Hebrew names. . . . It was not until the turn of the 18th century that there appeared the Sefer Hahayiim

---

1. Marcus, *Communal Sick-Care in the German*, 228.

which was to become one of the most popular works of this type.[2]

Maavor Yabok

Of the two texts under consideration, *Maavor Yabok* is the earlier. It was published in 1626 in Mantua, Italy. Its author was Aaron Berechiah ben Moses of Modena, who died in 1639. Marcus mentions that the book's date and Italian origin suggest that it was under the early influence of the *Chevra Kadisha* and their kabbalistic rituals and liturgies for the sick and dying.

From the prefatory remarks to the *Maavor Yabok* and Berechiah's own introduction, there seems to have been a group of Mantuans who cared for the sick and dying. This group appears under the name of מאירי השחר (*Meirei HaShachar*).[3] Berechiah first published a book for this group entitled משמרת הבוקר (*Mishmeret HaBoker*) in 1624. The book is composed of various prayers and biblical readings to be read each day by this group of early risers, however, as less than ten pages of this book are devoted to prayers for the sick and dying, it is not a manual to be of help to those who are going through these life experiences. In *Maavor Yabok*, both in the liturgical and explanatory sections, Berechiah does refer to this earlier work.

Regarding the practice of these rituals and prayers in Mantua and the work of the *Chevra Kadisha*, with which Berechiah came into contact, and explaining why he wrote this work, he writes:

> Oh, how happy I am but to be these few days in glorious Mantua, in the midst of this holy community, and with the congregations of Italy. . . . I have seen how many of the people correct their past deeds, and how many make their crooked paths straight by taking care of the dead and participating as members in groups of Gemilut Hasadim. But also, there are many of them who are not

2. Marcus, *Communal*, 228–230.

3. Berechiah b. Moses of Modena, *Maavor Yabok*, 6.

involved in Mishnah, Gemara, and Halacha, and who are not engaged in every aspect of the great commandment of taking care of the dead. I recently overheard that the community desired that one of its members undertake the task of arranging for them a prayerbook, so that they could join in song and prayer at the time of the going out of the soul.[4]

As to his ultimate desire for *Maavor Yabok*, Berechiah writes:

I composed new ideas and different explanations . . . to offer them as an offering and as incense in love and in reverence before the holy congregations, in order that it will make a way in the midst of the shaking worlds, . . . a bridge from the world of change and destruction with its sinful heavenly condition to be joined with the pleasures of Unity, Blessing, and Holiness . . . and will pass the fjord of Yabok to wrestle with the Lord, a man of war, until the dawn, that is resurrection for then our soul and body will no longer be called Jacob, but rather Israel, in that we will be a kingdom of priests and we will be worthy of seeing God face to face.[5]

These remarks and others in the introduction imply that the community, and the charitable groups in particular, were in need of a direction that an authoritative manual would supply. Berechiah saw his work as fulfilling this purpose. In his introduction, Berechiah does not mention a previous tradition in which a special significance was attached to the phrase "Maavor Yabok." This phrase comes from Genesis 33:22. It was the fjord over which Jacob "brought his family to safety, before going to meet his brother Esau." As to the significance of this title in the thematic development of the book, Berechiah writes:

in the first section a man will learn to awaken his creator by confession, prayer, and repentance as demonstrated by the *yod* of Yabok, that refers to the word (*Yichud*) יחוד. The second section is to bring a blessing to the soul and

4. Berechiah, *Maavor*, 19
5. Berechiah, *Maavor*, 14.

body . . . as demonstrated by the *bet* of Yabok, that refers
to the word (*Berachah*) ברכה. And by the third section
a man will sanctify himself . . . the *kof* of *Yabok* refers to
the word (*Kedushah*) קדושה.[6]

In this book, the word "section" refers to more than just a
"part" of the book: it refers to a "theme," because each section has a
different theme. *Maavor Yabok* is divided into five parts, however.
This first part, *Siftei Tzedek*, will be the one that will be analyzed
and used in this book, *Jewish Wisdom for Living and Dying*.

The fives parts are entitled:

1. שפתי צדק (*Siftei Tzedek*)

2. שפת אמת (*Sifat Emet*)

3. שפתי רננות (*Siftei Ranenut*)

4. עתר ענן הקטרת, קרבן תענית, מנחת אהרון (*Atar Anan HaKe-toret, Karban Taanit, Minchat Aharon*), and

5. אמרי נועם (*Emrei Noam*)

Sefer HaHayiim

Simon Frankfurter of Amsterdam, the author of *Sefer HaHayiim*,
was born in Schwerin, Poland, and died in 1712 in Amsterdam.
The first edition of the book was printed in 1703 in two volumes,
under the titles of *Dine Semahot* and *Alle Denims von Freuden*. The
second edition was printed in 1716 in one volume, by Simon's son
Moses. The third edition was printed in 1717.

From Frankfurter's history, as presented in his introduction,
he left Poland in 1656 as the result of a decree of death issued by
the government. Whether this was issued against him or against
his community is not stated. He fled to Amsterdam, where he
remained with writer Rabbi Benjamin Jedid from Frankfort. He
married Benjamin's daughter and was brought into the former's
group of *Gemilut Hasidim*, the *Chevra Kadisha*, doing good works.

---

6. Berechiah, *Maavor*, 16.

After thirty-eight years in this group, Simon began to study the works of the Geonim, of the various groups of *Chevra Kadisha*, and rabbinic texts, as well as those of the Kabbalah such as the *Zohar*.[7] He then collected these studies into his work, which was called *Sefer HaHayiim*.

The comparatively late date of Frankfurter's work, and that he lived most of his life in northern Europe, unlike Berechiah who lived in southern Europe, seem to point to a different social background for the sources of *Maavor Yabok* and *Sefer HaHayiim*. The sources might be different in that they would be affected by various customs pertaining to the sick and dying in their communities.

Like Berechiah, in stating why he felt the need to author this book, Frankfurter describes the community in the following manner:

> And my children, my people, are scattered in farms and towns, and they do not study in the way of kindness and truth. And there is no one to teach them.[8]

He also describes how they were lacking in the knowledge and customs of dealing with the dying and the dead. His function, as he saw it, was to teach people how to perform these duties. As his son wrote, "My father and teacher was aroused, and composed Sefer HaHayiim for the use of the dead and the living. [9]

As to Frankfurter's purpose in choosing the title *Sefer HaHayiim*, it is written in the introduction to *Andachts-Buch*:

> And he called it *Sefer Hahayiim*, in order that each man who desired life will be made worthy of it; as he wrote in the introduction to his book: 'And therefore I called the book of the law of kindness and truth, *Sefer Hahayiim*, that by it he will be worthy of being written in the book of life and will have the fear of heaven.'[10]

---

7. Rehfuss, *Andachts-Buch*, xviii.
8. Frankfurter, *Sefer HaHayiim*, introduction.
9. Frankfurter, *Sefer HaHayiim*, introduction.
10. Rehfuss, *Andachts-Buch*, xviii.

Sefer Hahayiim is entirely a liturgical work with some explanatory notes concerning customs and prayers interspersed throughout the book. Unlike *Maavor Yabok*, *Sefer Hahayiim* is not divided into various sections and chapters, but is presented as a unified liturgical handbook divided only by subtitles. In my analysis and discussion of these two books, the major liturgical sections in *Maavor Yabok* will be compared with their counterpart in *Sefer HaHayiim*, looking at the timeline from sickness to death

The prayers under discussion will be taken in the order in which they appear in their books. During my analysis and presentation of the rituals, prayers, and commentaries by the books' two authors, I will also discuss how these can be used in the modern context of visiting and caring for the sick and the dying.

Chapter II

<hr>

The Rabbinic View
of Sickness and Death

BOTH BOOKS, *MAAVOR YABOK* and *Sefer HaHayiim*, are founded on the themes of illness, death, and the afterlife, as found in rabbinic literature. Before delving into these books, it would be valuable to see what rabbinic literature has to say about these themes. This will then give the following discussion a basis for comparison regarding how these two books depend on or depart from the rabbinic treatment of these subjects.

Found in the midrashim, Mishnah, Talmud, and other rabbinic works, there was a direct relationship among sin, sickness, death, and the justice of God. The relationship between sin and death is described by S. Schechter, who writes:

> The identification of the Evil Yezer with the Angel of Death is sometimes modified in the sense of the former being the cause of death consequent upon sin rather than of his performing the office of the executioner. . . . But it must be noted that in other places it is sin itself that causes death. 'See, my children,' said the saint R. Chaninah b. Dosa to his disciples,' it is not the ferocious ass that kills, it is sin that kills.'[1]

<hr>

1. Schechter, *Aspects of Rabbinic Theology*, 245–247.

Rabbi Akiba was known to have believed that one should not fight against sufferings (sickness and loss), but rather, should accept them, as no one is free from sin.[2]

This statement implies a relationship between sin and sickness and God's justice. This knowledge of God's justice, in God's dealings with people, was essential to the rabbinic system. The phrase צידוק הדין (*Tziduk HaDin*) taken from Deuteronomy 32:4 was used by the rabbis in haggadic, liturgical, and halachic statements. Schechter quotes the rabbis when he writes:

> 'He sits in judgment against everyone and gives one what is due to him.' It is with reference to the same verse (Deut. 32:4) that a later Rabbi makes the remark to the effect: He who says the Holy One, blessed be He (or the Merciful One), is loose (or lax) in his dealing out justice, let his life become loose. He is long-suffering but collects his (debt), in the end.[3]

It is through a system of justice that God first rules the world. "For God is not suspected to execute judgment without justice."[4] There is, among the rabbis, emphasis on the quality of judgment, מידת הדין (*Midat HaDin*). However, they formulate, as part of their system the concept of the quality of mercy, מידת הרחמים (*Midat HaRachamim*). As Schechter writes:

> Death and suffering may be viewed either as a punishment satisfying the claims of justice, or as an atonement, bringing pardon and forgiveness and reconciling man with God.[5]

Schechter seems to imply that suffering as punishment and suffering as atonement are two sides of the same coin. This paradox can be seen in the following rabbinic remark:

> 'They asked Wisdom (Hagiographa), 'What is the punishment of the sinner? Wisdom answered, 'Evil pursues

2. Urbach, *The Sages*, 392
3. Schechter, *Aspects*, 306.
4. Schechter, *Aspects*, 307.
5. Schechter, *Aspects*, 304.

sinners' (Prov. 13:2). They asked Prophecy, . . . Prophecy answered, 'The soul that sinneth, it shall die' (Ezek. 18:4). They asked the Torah . . . Torah answered, 'Let him bring a guilt-offering and it shall be forgiven unto him, as it is said, 'And it shall be accepted for him to make an atonement for him.'[6]

In one sense, God's mercy can be seen, in the rabbinic system, as a function of God's justice. God acts mercifully when a person's deeds warrant this mercy. But the rabbis also had a conception of unmerited mercy, which goes under the name "Sufferings out of Love," ייסורין של אהבה (*Yesurin Shel Ahavah*). However, whether mercy is a function of merited or unmerited deeds, repentance, and confession influences God's mercy, and thus can offset sin, sickness, and death. G. Moore, in his book *Judaism*, writes:

> In accordance with this, later authorities teach that even those sins which ipso facto exclude the sinner from a share in the World to Come, do so only in case he dies without repentance. If he turns from wickedness and dies in a state of repentance, he is one of the children of the World to Come, for there is nothing that can stand before repentance.[7]

The rabbis saw suffering and death as means in themselves for atonement. Suffering, if accepted by the sufferer, leads to confession of sins, and therefore is as a sacrificial offering before God. The acceptance of suffering becomes a positive move towards overcoming suffering, whether it is suffering, sickness, or death. This is possible because the acceptance of suffering, and therefore repentance, changes the divine decree. Schechter in his analysis of the rabbinic sources finds:

> 'Beloved is suffering, for as sacrifices are atoning, so is suffering atoning.' Nay, suffering has even a greater atoning effect than sacrifice, in as much as sacrifice affects only man's property, whilst suffering touches his very self. . . This suffering has to be a sacrifice accompanied

6. Schechter, *Aspects,* 293.
7. Moore, *Judaism,* I, 521.

by repentance. The sufferer has to accept the suffer-
ing—prayerfully and in a spirit of submission and has to
recognize that the visitation of God was merited by him.
Man knows well in his heart when weighing his deeds
with the suffering which came upon him that he was
dealt with mercifully.[8]

Not only is repentance a means to annul God's decrees: so,
too, are good deeds, prayer, and study. All of these come under the
heading of atonement. Other rabbinic sources state:

Prayer, charity, and repentance, these three together
avert the impending doom. [9]

Atoning powers are ascribed also to the study of the Law,
which is more effective than sacrifice, especially when
combined with good works.[10]

The goal of this process from sickness to atonement,
according to the rabbinical view, can be seen as a "...
regeneration-restoration of the original state of man in
his relation to God, called tekanah." [11]

Finally, confession itself is so potent in influencing God's
decree, the Day of Atonement becomes a paradigm for this act of
confession: that is, atonement.

All the various elements affecting atonement are in a
marked degree combined in the Day of Atonement, to
make it the occasion of the great annual reintegration of
man. [12]

The Day of Atonement is seen as influencing atonement and
thus God's decree of judgement and mercy; the day of death is also
seen this way. This connection between the two days is stressed in
the Mishnah, Yoma 8:8: "The Sin-offering and the unconditional

8. Schechter, *Aspects*, 309.
9. *Jewish Encyclopedia*, II, 279.
10. Jewish *Encyclopedia*, II, 279.
11. *Jewish Encyclopedia*, II 280.
12. *Jewish Encyclopedia*, II 280.

Guilt-offering affect atonement; death and the Day of Atonement affect atonement if there is repentance." This statement from the Mishnah could influence the similarity between liturgies for the deathbed and the Day of Atonement because they have similar goals.

From these various rabbinic statements, it can be seen how the rabbis viewed the experiences of the sick and dying. Sickness and death are seen as the judgments of God. They represent breaks in one's relationship with God. These are judgments caused by sin, but they are also instrumental in moving a person to atonement. Acceptance of judgment, repentance, study, prayer, and good deeds then become strategies for atonement that can change God's decrees by moving God to mercy. Whereas justice is seen as the overriding principle, mercy is the part of the system by which a person can move back into a favorable relationship with God.

Changing the decree of God can bring about healing as well as an escape from death. On the other hand, if death must come, it is part of the atonement strategy to overcome death by the reward of an eternal life in the "World to Come," *Olam Ha-Bah*. If these changes are achieved by these strategies, which are based on acceptance of one's sickness and death (one's suffering), then acceptance is not passive, but rather, a continually active move on the part of the sick person.

This then is the rabbinic foundation upon which both Berechiah and Frankfurter built their manuals.

Chapter III

~~~~~~

INTRODUCTORY PRAYERS AND MEDITATIONS FOR THE SICK

Now, JOIN WITH ME on a journey through the sections of *Sefer HaHayiim* and then *Maavor Yabok*, as they describe the various rituals and prayers from sickness till death. As I read the texts themselves, I try to put myself in the place of the one who is ill or dying, as well as the place of the visitor. This helps me to understand and appreciate the words better. This also allows me to be open to the spiritual effect of these words of Frankfurter and Berechiah in the hope that I can then apply these spiritual teachings to rituals and prayers I might perform today. This personal interaction with these texts integrates them into the very being of the reader to either be used or rejected. I ask you to do the same.

Let us begin!

Sefer HaHayiim

Sefer HaHayiim has an introductory section of five sedarim, or sections. Each section is to be read on a different day of a person's illness or during the period of mourning. The sections are composed of quotations mostly from the Torah, Talmud, and Midrash. The main thrust of these readings is given in the introductory remark:

'The law of the Lord is perfect, restoring the soul,' the soul of the living and the dying. The wise will study with the sick, after their prayers, each seder, as this is part of the basis of Sefer HaHayiim. He also needs to study, with the mourner, one chapter from the five chapters each one of the seven days of mourning. And the sick will pay attention to their prayers and their study.[1]

This remark points out that study with the sick is of utmost importance. Study is placed on an equal degree of importance with prayer. I have translated the word מתים (*meytim*) as "dying," and not as "dead," because the wise cannot go and study with the dead, but only with the dying. In context, therefore, the word "dying" makes better sense than does the word "dead."

This opening remark of Frankfurter immediately presents a method for how one should visit the sick that is radically different from a modern approach to this task. The emphasis today is on counseling, which entails either a "listening" or a "directive" approach, or at least developing a supportive and caring relationship with the patient. If a clergy, a member of a *Chevra Kadisha*, or a friend is making the visit, a prayer might be said on the sick person's behalf or said together with him or her. There might even be study of a religious text, but this would not necessarily be offered at the beginning of the visit or the main goal of the visit, unless the patient gives permission either verbally or silently to do so. In Frankfurter's time, these rituals and prayers as options were probably not available to the visitor. As will be seen in this analysis of the texts, the obligation of the visitor was straight forward; to pray for mercy for the sick person and to help him confess his sins.

Various inspirational texts from the tradition are then presented to reinforce this function of the visitor, regarding the visiting procedure.

The introductory remark to the second part of the first section is:

I am convinced that upon mercy is the Universe established. That mercy is one of the things by which a man

1. Frankfurter, *Sefer* 1a

will eat of the fruits in this world, and the capital is to be established in the world to come.[2]

The texts quoted in this part of the book tell of the importance of dealing with mercy in relationships among people. Such relationships are termed גמילות חסדים (*gemilut hasadim*), which is translated in one of the English editions as "disinterested benevolence."[3] They are benevolent deeds because they are for the good of another, and they are done with disinterest, meaning that they are not done for the sake of reward.

This sense of mercy is learned from God's dealings with people according to *Sefer HaHayiim*. These deeds of גמילות חסדים (*gemilut hasadim*)include visiting the sick and those in mourning. Passages are quoted that teach that a sense of mercy is a prerequisite for visiting the unfortunate and the sick, and those in mourning. In visiting the sick, although God's mercy upon the sick person can be accessed through prayer, it is also brought into the room when the visitor acts with compassion, understanding, and open-mindedness. In this way, there is a similarity between modern visiting practices and those described here from *Sefer HaHayiim*. As one such modern counseling textbook states:

> Now the religious leader shares with the psychiatrist and the caseworker an attitude of sympathy and respect for the individual—and for his family—but his relationship to him differs from theirs as it is based upon ambiguous faith and a spiritual interpretation of man and society.[4]

The text of *Sefer HaHayiim* that is quoted begins "We find concerning the deed of Rabbi Perachyah in *Midrash Hanne'lan Ruth*"[5], is from a mystical source. R. Perachyah is shown the Garden of Eden with its 365 palaces because he led his life with mercy. He then becomes an exemplar of behavior. This is one of the few

---

2. Frankfurter, *Sefer*, 12b.

3. Ascher, *The Book of Life and Expression of the Tongue*, 7.

4. Linn and Schwartz, *Psychiatry and Religious Experience*, 104.

5. Frankfurter, *Sefer*, 3b

quotations from a mystical source in this introductory section and therefore should be noted.

The final part of the first section is introduced by the exclamation "The mercy of God endures continually."[6] This part repeats the idea, stated earlier, that a person practices mercy as that person senses God's mercy upon the person. As stated in the first paragraph of this part:

> that man ought to be mindful of the mercies of God. . . .
> Man is, therefore, in duty bound to walk in the ways of
> God, and continually practice [*sic*] virtue and mercy to
> mankind, without distinction.[7]

The second section begins with the following verse from the psalms: "The prayer of the afflicted when he is overwhelmed, and poureth out his complaint before the Eternal."[8] This part of the second section speaks of the value of prayer, but especially during sickness and danger. Here, God is called the "heavenly physician."[9] Therefore, prayer can call for God's protection from sickness, which is seen as a chastisement from God, and is also able to bring about an easy death. Such a death is seen as a tranquil sleep and is described as "the kiss of death." Prayer, according to these passages, silences judgments against the sick person. As the sick person prays and turns to God, protection then follows.

This part is interesting considering the modern question of "to tell or not to tell?" A person should know of the reality of impending death so that this person can turn to God by prayer, and thus be saved. The process of *Teshuvah*, repentance, can begin only with acceptance of one's action, sin, and the desire to repair that sin. Unlike the first section, the direction presented is more to the sick person than to the visitor, because preparing for the reality of sickness and death by prayer and confession can aid the person in being saved from either or both.

6. Frankfurter, *Sefer*, 3b
7. Ascher, *The Book of Life*, 19.
8. Ascher, *The Book of Life*, 21.
9. Ascher, *The Book of Life*, 21.

The second part of this section begins with the biblical verse: "Surely the bitterness of death is gone."[10] This part adds repentance, study of Torah, and deeds of Loving Kindness גמילות חסדים to prayer as ways in which a person can influence God to be saved from death. These various strategies, by which one can be saved from sickness and death, have a biblical basis in the story of King Hezekiah. They enable one to avert the decrees of God, because:

> Our sages also teach that by four means man may avert the pending punishment: viz. charity, devout prayer, amending his past conduct, and by acquiring an exemplary name. [11]

The reality of death is stressed in a quotation from Talmud *Avodah Zara*,[12] which depicts impressive images of death. The purpose of this presentation is to get the reader to turn to God and to receive the "kiss of death," an easy death, which awaits the dying patient. These strategies present the sick and dying person with an active rather than a passive role in the face of these calamities.

The first part of the third section begins: "Good and upright is the Eternal; therefore, He will teach sinners in the way."[13] This section underscores God's exactness in dealing with a person, because God teaches a person to do good and to shun the bad. The goal of sickness and death is to get a person to turn again to God.

The rabbis quoted here answer the question of theodicy by saying that what are apparent evils, sickness, and death, are good, because they benefit a person in either this world or the next. "Whilst He corrects by lenient chastisement, He exalts at the same time, by making man mindful of his sins, and causing him to repent."[14]

God's justice becomes the overriding principle. One way this is reconciled with God's mercy is seen in the following:

10. Ascher, *The Book of Life*, 27
11. Ascher, *The Book of Life*, 29
12. Ascher, *The Book of Life*, 27
13. Ascher, *The Book of Life*, 33.
14. Ascher, *The Book of Life*, 33.

Rabb Eliezer calls our attention to the apparent contradiction in the above verse, the former part of which says, 'And unto Thee, O Eternal, belongeth mercy' whilst the latter part says, 'For Thou renderest to every man according to his work;' which the Rabbi thus reconciles: The reward according to our deeds precedes, and the mercy of the Eternal follows.'[15]

It is hoped that a person awakens himself to repentance, but if he does not, God uses dreams and then chastisements to teach God's ways.[16] These ways will then lead the person to repent.

This part then presents the sick or dying person with religious answers as to God's relationship to the person's sickness and/or approaching death. Such answers may have the goal of moving the sick or dying person to use one of the strategies mentioned earlier. Such chastisements by God, sickness, and death, have that goal. Therefore, if a sick or dying person uses these strategies, he or she will be in line with God's goals and receive the benefits of Divine justice and mercy. Described in this part, we find presentation of numerous tools that include prayers and rituals available for use by sick or dying people in the face of such events.

The second part of this third section begins with the verse: "Woe unto the wicked sinner; for the reward of his hands shall be given him."[17] This section describes the man or woman who fails to heed God's warnings, and consequently what will happen to that person. He will fall prey to sickness and death. However, it is stressed that repentance is always possible, even at the last minute before death.[18]

The first part of the fourth section begins: "For whom the Eternal loveth, He correcteth."[19] This section attempts to demonstrate that because God's chastisements come from God's love to correct a person, that person must accept them as such and turn

15. Ascher, *The Book of Life*, 35.

16. Ascher, *The Book of Life*, 36

17. Ascher, *The Book of Life*, 41.

18. Ascher, *The Book of Life*, 44,45.

19. Ascher, *The Book of Life*, 45.

from sin. According to this idea, we find the following observation by Ravah:

> Ravah observes: 'Whoever submits to Divine punishment with pious resignation, will behold his offspring enjoying long life. . . . The Holy One (blessed be He) visits at times with the greatest rigour the most immaterial trespasses of His pious men, in order to cleanse their souls from all iniquity, so that they may enter in perfect purity the gates of everlasting felicity.[20]

This acceptance of God's chastisements must be understood to be active, not passive. Acceptance does not mean resignation in the negative sense of the word. Acceptance of God's chastisements is a positive efficacious act. This act can even affect the change of God's decrees because it is considered an act of repentance. This is just another strategy available for sick or dying people.

The second part of this fourth section begins: "There is a time to be born and a time to die."[21]

This part stresses an awareness that death does come, and that all people need to live a good life and be repentant. It is stated that one should return to God before death. Consolation for dying people at the time of death comes with the knowledge of a future life for those who have turned to God.

> Yet be not terrified, son of man, at that awful hour. Be rather consoled, for the Eternal is good to all, and His compassion extends to all His creatures; yea all His doings are mercy and truth; all that the Holy One (blessed be He) hath created is merely for the sake of the righteous man, in order to do good unto him at his latter end, and that his soul may reach its destination in eternal bliss. Thus, we see how man ought to purify his thoughts, and even at his dying hour praise and acknowledge the justice of God; so that his soul may quit its earthly abode in purity and innocence . . .[22]

20. Ascher, *The Book of Life*, 47.
21. Ascher, *The Book of Life*, 59.
22. Ascher, *The Book of Life*, 60,61.

The fifth section begins with the following directive: "Visit the sick, and endeavor to alleviate their distress."[23] This section, as the first one, is written for the visitor. It tells of both the details and rewards of visiting the sick. The latter part of this section is devoted to the rewards of taking care of the dead and visiting the mourners.

Because this section and the previous section attempt to tell the visitor of his rewards for visiting, we learn that one visits not only for the sake of the person being visited, but also for himself or herself.

In conclusion of these introductory sections from *Sefer HaHayiim*, it should be noted that these readings from rabbinic sources are read and studied in a fixed sequence, as if they were a fixed liturgy. They are studied by the visitor and the visited person for the benefit of both. There are passages that compare study with prayer, implying that study is a guide to correct behavior and a source of comfort to the distressed, but it is also as efficacious as prayer.

Whereas the concept of God's mercy is discussed in the second section, the third and fourth sections point out that God's justice and judgment precede God's mercy. The relationship between God and a person in the presence of sickness, dying, and death, as found in this introductory section, is marked by a sense of God's overriding justice, which includes divine mercy. A final comment is that of seventy-eight paragraphs in these sections, only two, the twenty-third and twenty-fourth paragraphs, contain quotations from the kabbalistic literature. Such a small number of quotations from this literature implies a reliance upon rabbinic material.

Maavor Yabok

The section of *Maavor Yabok* that deals with visitation of the sick begins by presenting eight sections to be read in a fixed order each day during the time of sickness. As in the introductory section in

23. Ascher, *The Book of Life*, 65.

Sefer HaHayiim, the section here is composed of readings. However, these readings are from the *Tanach*, bible, and not rabbinic sources.

Each section in this part is introduced by five verses from the *Tanach* and concludes with three paragraphs composed of various biblical verses.

The introductory paragraph to these sections is:

> We beseech You, Adonai, save now (three times) (Ps 118:25)
>
> Hear my prayer, Adonai, and give ear to my cry; Keep not silence at my tears; For I am a stranger with You, A sojourner, as all my ancestors were. (Ps 39:13) Like a swallow or a crane, so do I chatter, I do moan as a dove; My eyes fail with looking upward. O Adonai, You be my surety (Is 38:14) For the nether-world cannot praise You, Death cannot celebrate You; They that go down into the pit cannot hope for Your truth (Is 38:18) Adonai is ready to save me; Therefore we will sing songs to the stringed instruments All the days of our life in the house of Adonai (Is 38:20) Forsake me not, Adonai; O my God be not far from me (Ps 38:22) Make haste to help me, O Adonai, my salvation (Ps 38:23)[24]

These verses ask for God's salvation and answer to prayer. The worshipper speaks of himself or herself as a sojourner, a wanderer, searching for God. The verse from Is. 38:18 is used as an argument against God. The reader wants to know whether God would let him die, death being a state in which he cannot praise God. It ends with the petition for God's closeness and salvation. These verses depict the sick one as a lost person searching for a relationship with God, who is this person's salvation. The goal is that death should not come at all, because it, as well as sickness, represents this breach between man and God.

It is then stated that each section is to be concluded with three paragraphs. Here is the first:

---

24. Berechiah, *Maavor*, 56,57.

That Your beloved may be delivered, Save with Your right hand, and answer me (Ps 60:7) Behold, O God our shield, and look upon the face of Your anointed (Ps 84:10) I shall not die, but live, And declare the works of Adonai. Adonai has chastened me sore; But God has not given me over to death (Ps 118:17,18) For in death there is no remembrance of You; In the nether-world who will give You thanks? (Ps 6:6) Shall Your mercy be declared in the grave? Or Your faithfulness in destruction? Shall Your wonders be known in the dark? And Your righteousness in the land of forgetfulness? (Ps 88:12,13) Will You work wonders for the dead? Or shall the shades arise and give You thanks? Selah (Ps 88:11) The dead praise not Adonai, Neither any that go down into silence; But we will bless Adonai from this time forth and forever. Hallelujah. (Ps 115:17,18) What profit is there in my blood, when I go down to the pit? Shall the dust praise You? Shall it declare Your truth? (Ps 30:10) For the nether world cannot praise You, Death cannot celebrate You; They that go down into the pit cannot hope for Your truth. The living, the living, he shall praise You, As I do this day; The father to the children shall make known Your truth (Is 38:18,19)[25]

As with the earlier introductory passage, this first paragraph of the eight sections presents verses demonstrating how, in death, a person cannot praise God. These verses would console a sick person because he or she would realize that God wants a person's praise, and therefore would want the person to live, as the last verse declares. For a dying person, these verses might also hint at an eternal life, as well as recovery from illness. If death and destruction are overcome by eternal life, praises can still be sung in God's presence as they were sung in life.

The following is the second paragraph:

Then say three times:
Heal me, Adonai, and I shall be healed; Save me, and I shall be saved; For You are my praise (Jer. 17:14) Bring me forth out of the net that they have hidden for me;

25. Berechiah, *Maavor,* 59,60.

For You are my stronghold. Into Your hand I commit my spirit; You have redeemed me, Adonai, You God of truth (Ps 31:5,6) Adonai bless you, and keep you; Adonai make God's face to shine upon you and be gracious unto you; Adonai lift up God's countenance upon you, and give you peace (Nu 6:24–26) For Your salvation, I wait, Adonai. I wait, Adonai, For Your salvation. Adonai, For Your salvation, I wait (Gen 49:18) For Your salvation, I wait, Adonai. I wait, Adonai, For Your salvation. Adonai, For Your salvation, I wait. (Aramaic translation of previous) You are my hiding-place; You will preserve me from the adversary; With songs of deliverance, You will surround me (Ps 32:7) On my right side the angel Michael. On my left side the angel Gavriel. Before me, the angel Raphael. Behind me the angel Nuriel and upon my head the Divine Presence of God. Bless is Adonai in the day. Blessed is Adonai at night. Blessed is Adonai in our lying down and blessed is Adonai is our rising up.[26]

Most of these verses are taken from the liturgical readings from the bedtime ritual entitled "Saying the Shema on One's Bed." The verses ask for God's healing, salvation, blessing, and protection. These verses also emphasize a relationship with God as being the ideal state. The final paragraph of this concluding section continues the already expressed idea of the sick one's hope in the Lord, that God will release the person from pain and tears. Note the use of the words כאבי (*kaavi*), דמעתי (*dimati*) and בכיי (*b'chi*), "My pain," "My tears," and "My cries." These are certainly words expressive of the emotive and physical experiences of the sick person and thereby words that a sick person can relate to in his or her prayers.

The verse "The Lord of hosts, happy is the man who trusts in Adonai" would certainly be a comfort to its reader. It says in essence that God is with those who turn toward to God. The final paragraph of this section reads:

Bind up my wounds. My Rock and My Light. My thoughts are to You to alleviate my pain. I alone look to

26. Berechiah, *Maavor*, 60.

Your Name that You heal me. To You God I place my
hope with all my hear. Turn away from me those who
wish harm. Hear my voice, my cry Adonai. You have
counted my wanderings; You put my tears into Your
bottle; Are they not in Your book? (Ps 56:9) The Lord of
hosts is with us; The God of Jacob is our high tower (Ps.
46:8) O Adonai of hosts, Happy is the person that trusts
in You (Ps. 84:13) Adonai, save O ruler! Answer us on
the day we call! (Ps 20:10) Let the words of my mouth
and the meditation of my heart be acceptable before You,
Adonai, my Rock, and my Redeemer. (Ps 19:15)[27]

Just as these verses from the *Tanach* make up the content of
the introduction and conclusion to the eight sections to be read
each day, verses from *Tanach* also make up the content of the sec-
tions themselves. Each section has six verses from Torah, twelve
verses from Prophets, and eighteen verses from the Writings.

Although *Sefer HaHayiim* states that it is efficacious for the
sick person to study, it especially emphasizes the study of rabbinic
literature. *Maavor Yabok* also sees the efficaciousness of study be-
cause it, too, places study into a liturgical framework, but study
is seen here as study of the *Tanach*, and particularly study of the
Psalms. *Maavor Yabok*, just as *Sefer HaHayiim*, suggests that the
one who visits should study with the sick one, which certainly falls
within the role of the pastoral visit of today.

> The one who visits the sick, the sage, will make him un-
> derstand man's latter end, and he will give thanks and
> praise of the Living One, and he will petition his King.
> And the father will inform the children, and he will teach
> them to petition God by words of Tanach because behold
> the Lord stands upon the wall of the Tanach, as a fortress
> in times of trouble.[28]

As to the function and purpose of the study of *Tanach*, al-
though both works see them as efficacious, their descriptions of
the process of "influencing the Divine" are different.

27. Berechiah, *Maavor*, 60.
28. Berechiah, *Maavor*, 54.

Sefer HaHayiim, in quoting from rabbinic texts, describes the study of *Tanach* during the time of sickness in terms of rewards that are viewed as health, the length of days, peace, and eternal life:

> Rabbi Simon, son of Yochai, says ... But even the patient himself must not neglect to embrace the moment, whilst it is yet in his power, to pour forth his heart in supplication before the Holy One (blessed be He), and to render himself worthy of God's mercy by meditation on the divine law; limited as his meditation may be, it only requires to flow from a devout heart. And we read in the Talmud Berachoth, fol. v.p.1: 'Meditation on the divine law affords relief from the severest afflictions . . .'[29]

> Hence it follows that they who themselves study, and the supporters of those who exclusively devote their time to study, are equally meritorious, and both may expect great reward . . .[30]

> And thus says King Solomon: 'My son, forget not my law . . . then shalt thou walk in thy way safely. . . . For length of days, and a happy and peaceful life shall it add unto thee. It shall be health to thy flesh, and marrow to thy bones. Hear, my son, and receive my sayings, and the years of thy life shall be many. For they are life unto those that find them, and health to all their flesh. . . . And God himself said: 'For this (the law) is thy life, and the length of thy days.'[31]

> The study of the law is also accompanied with another blessing – that of peace, as we read: 'All thy children shall be taught of the Eternal, and great shall be the peace of thy children . . .'[32]

29. Ascher, *The Book of Life*, 1.
30. Ascher, *The Book of Life*, 2.
31. Ascher, *The Book of Life*, 3.
32. Ascher, *The Book of Life*, 3,4.

> For Scripture says: 'They (the moral doctrines) shall be
> an ornament of grace unto thy head, and a diadem about
> thy neck.'[33]

Rabbi Isaac says:

> He who studies the biblical portions which treat of the
> laws and ceremonies of the sin- offerings and the guilt-
> offerings, will be deemed by the Eternal as if he actually
> brought those sacrifices; for Scripture says: 'This is the
> law of the sin-offering.'[34]

These rabbinic statements describe in precise terms the effect
of study: that is, its rewards. They do not go into a discussion as to
the precise process of study's effect upon sickness or how a person
influences the Divine by such study, which then brings on healing.
They only imply that the process is based on the idea of Divine
reward and punishment. This is based on a person's actions, how
the study of the law can bring relief from afflictions, and that the
lack of such study will cause one to "more sorely feel the heavy
pangs with which he will be visited."[35]

Maavor Yabok, on the other hand, writes of the effect and
process of study upon the Divine in a different manner using the
teachings found in the kabbalistic sources:

> And by these verses the gates of mercy open, all of them
> together. They are of the number thirty-six, each one
> equivalent to the three sources of the attributes of mercy
> suspended in the summits of the turnings of the heart
> and soul. They draw the source of life from the hidden
> knowledge sealed above and from hidden knowledge be-
> low. Therefore, they are two times eighteen that is 'Life,
> Life' חי. He will praise and bless you, and from there He
> will inspire health and healing by the Exalted Will which
> pours forth from the Possessor of the Exalted Will upon
> each blessing and praise, My mouth will speak the praise

33. Ascher, *The Book of Life*, 4.
34. Ascher, *The Book of Life*, 5.
35. Ascher, *The Book of Life*, 1,2.

of the Lord and He will bless all flesh, the name of His holiness is forever and forever.[36]

It is evident that study is seen by the author of *Maavor Yabok* as more than just a correct religious commandment to be fulfilled within the halachic, legal, system, which then is followed by a respective reward or punishment from God. Rather, it is a religiously commanded act directly affecting the divine flow of mercy through the divine energy levels called *Sefirot* from the second *Sefirah* of *Hochmah*, Knowledge. There is an actual description of the metaphysical process at work demonstrating how study of holy text can affect wellness.

The kabbalistic language is evident here. In addition, there is present theosophical knowledge of how study influences the godhead. Such knowledge is absent from *Sefer HaHayiim*'s rabbinic quotations. Also, in contrast to *Sefer HaHayiim*, most references in *Maavor Yabok* come from the *Zohar* and *Tekunei Ha-Zohar*.

Each of the eight sections in this introductory section in *Maavor Yabok* is composed of thirty-six verses. These are six verses from the Torah, twelve from the Prophets, and eighteen from the Writings. The number thirty-six is significant because it is double eighteen, which is equivalent to double חי (*chai*), or life. Most probably the number of verses was chosen for this reason.

As shown previously, the eight *sedarim* or sections from *Maavor Yabok* serve a similar function as do the reflections in *Sefer HaHayiim*. In both cases, they are verses to be studied and recited by the person who is ill. It would therefore be interesting to analyze the general contents of these *sedarim* and compare their thematic emphasis with the reflections in *Sefer HaHayiim*.

The first one begins with a listing of Psalms 13, 15, 16, and 17. The reader can choose one of these. Psalm 13 "opens on a note of despondency, passes on to prayer, hope, and a promise of thanksgiving."[37]

---

36. Berechiah, *Maavor*, 55.
37. Kissane, *The Book of Psalms*, I, 52.

The subject of Psalm 15 deals with the conduct required of the true Israelite and his consequent reward.[38] In Psalm 16, the psalmist "rejoices in his faith, for he is confident that Yahweh will shield him from disaster and give him a life of happiness."[39]

Also, in Psalm 16 the speaker prays for relief from suffering and from persecution by enemies who gloat over his mastery. He claims God's protection on two grounds: (a) he is free from sin in thought, word, and deed; and (b) he is a zealous follower of God's law, one of those who have confidence in the goodness and justice of God.[40]

Psalm 17 is "David's hymn of thanksgiving to God for his deliverance from all the perils which beset him during his life. . . ."[41]

As these psalms speak of God's salvation for one who hopes in God and follows God's ways, they establish the themes for these verses from the *Tanach* in this section. These themes of God's blessings and protection for those who trust in God are carried over into the verses from the Torah:

> Who is like unto Thee O Lord, who is like unto Thee, awesome in holiness, awesome in praises, working wonders. Thine right hand O Lord is my glory, by the strength of Thine right hand O Lord Thou wilt crush the enemy.[42]

From the Prophets,

> Behold the Lord is my salvation, I will be secure. I will not fear because my strength and song is Jah the Lord, and He will be for me my salvation.[43]

And from the Writings,

---

38. Kissane, *The Book of Psalms*, I, 59.

39. Kissane, *The Book of Psalms*, I, 59.

40. Kissane, *The Book of Psalms* I, 66.

41. Kissane, *The Book of Psalms* I, 72.

42. Berechiah, *Maavor*, 58.

43. Berechiah, *Maavor*, 58.

O Lord my God, in Thee I trust, save me from all those who pursue me, and save me.[44]

The second *seder* begins with Psalms 19, 20, 22, and 23. The subject of Psalm 19 is "the glory of Yahweh as manifested in the heavens and in the law."[45] Psalm 20 asks for the success of the king and his kingdom in the day of their trouble.[46]

Of Psalm 22,

> It is a prayer of one who is enduring intense suffering which has worn down his physical strength and brought him to the point of death. His weakness has left him an easy victim to his powerful foes, and he can look for no aid or comfort from his fellow-men. These merely look on and gloat over his misery, and calculate how they may profit by his death. Accustomed to regard suffering as the penalty of sin, he is perplexed by God's apparent abandonment of one who has always been a devoted servant and now has to bear the taunts of the unbeliever because of his piety. Yet in God is his only hope and he makes a fervent appeal for His aid before it is too late. He ends with a promise of solemn and public thanksgiving service in the Temple. [47]

It appears that the psalmist is appealing to God's mercy alone. The ways of justice and judgment, as described so directly in *Sefer HaHayiim* do not seem to be operative because this person is asking not to be judged according to his or her past deeds.

Psalm 23 describes the blessings enjoyed by the believer that will be received from God, who acts as a shepherd and a host.

After this opening section from Psalms, there is a section of other verses from the *Tanach*. First, a verse is quoted from the Hagar story that relates the protective quality of God over the unfortunate and over one's progeny:

44. Berechiah, *Maavor*, 59.
45. Kissane, *The Book of Psalms*, I, 83
46. Kissane, *The Book of Psalms*, I, 88–89.
47. Kissane, *The Book of Psalms*, I, 94.

> And God heard the voice of the child, and an angel of
> God called to Hagar from heaven, and said to her: 'What
> is with you Hagar, do not be afraid, for God has heard the
> voice of the child as he is there.'[48]

Sworn protection over the children of Abraham, Jacob, and
the people of Israel is also related in verses from the Torah.
Continuing the theme of these psalms, verses are quoted
from the Prophets that recall how God helps those in dire trouble:

> Be strong weak hands, strong weak knees. . . . But they
> that wait for the Lord shall renew their strength; they
> shall mount up with wings as eagles; they shall run and
> not be weary; they shall walk and not be afraid.[49]

The verses from the Writings continue this theme of Divine
protection, such as: "Thou hast given me Thy shield of salvation;
and Thy condescension hath made me great."[50]

All these verses have a psychologically positive influence of
comfort for the sick or dying. This comfort comes from promises
verbalized by these words. There is also the knowledge that such
verses bring one back into a relationship with God, whose benefits
will be described subsequently.

The third section begins with Psalms 24, 25, 28, and 30.

Psalm 24 is composed of three parts: (1) an introductory
hymn on the majesty of God; (2) a psalm on the character of
the true Israelite; and (3) a decalogue between the priest and the
people as the procession arrives at the Temple.[51]

Psalm 25 contains "prayers for guidance and protection, for
pardon from sin, for deliverance from trouble, and from the at-
tacks of enemies."[52] Verses 6 and 7, which are the verses in which
pardon from sin is asked, appeal to God's mercy, and not God's
justice:

48. Berechiah, *Maavor,* 62.

49. Berechiah, *Maavor,* 63.

50. Berechiah, *Maavor,* 63.

51. Kissane, *The Book of Psalms,* I, 106.

52. Kissane, *The Book of Psalms,* I, 110.

> Remember Thy compassion and Thy mercy, Yahweh, for they have been from olden time; the sins and transgressions of my youth remember not. According to Thy mercy do Thou remember me, for Thy goodness sake, Yahweh.[53]

In Psalm 28, the psalmist begs "Yahweh for aid, lest he die."[54] The one who languishes asks for judgment of the wicked and has confidence in this, because this person knows that "Yahweh is the protector of His people and of His king."[55]

Psalm 30 is a:

> Psalm of thanksgiving for recovery from sickness. After a brief introduction in which the psalmist announces his themes, he recalls his former happiness, his sudden affliction, his appeal to God for relief, and his recovery for which he now makes thanksgiving.[56]

The method of each section is that the opening psalms set the theme for the following verses from the *Tanach*. This was proven in the first two sections, and it is also true for the remaining six. This being the case, only the introductory psalms in the remaining *sedarim* will be summarized.

The fourth section includes Psalms 31, 38, 40, and 41 in its introduction.

The psalmist of Psalm 31

> reveals himself as one who is worn out by suffering . . . as little regarded as a dead man or a broken vessel. He is sustained by his belief in the goodness and justice of God, who has revealed Himself as the protector of the faithful, and whose favours he himself has experienced in the past.[57]

---

53. Berechiah, *Maavor*, 64.

54. Kissane, *The Book of Psalms*, I, 122.

55. Kissane, *The Book of Psalms*, I, 122.

56. Kissane, *The Book of Psalms*, I, 129.

57. Kissane, *The Book of Psalms*, I, 133.

Psalm 31 is somewhat different from the psalms discussed thus far. The writer begins by declaring that sufferings are due to God's chastisements and rebukes. God is then pictured in God's aspect of a stern judge. However, the Psalm concludes with an appeal to God's mercy as with the earlier psalms. "The psalmist acknowledges his guilt, but prays for mercy and deliverance from his suffering."[58]

In Psalm 40, the psalmist, who has many troubles, recalls a faithfulness to God and "is confident that in return God will not leave him without help in his present troubles."[59]

The writer of Psalm 41 "appeals to God to pardon his sins and restore him to health."[60]

The fifth section contains Psalms 42, 43, 51, and 61.

Psalms 42 and 43 tell of the psalmist's exile from Jerusalem, God's home. As is written in a commentary to these psalms: "Now he is in deepest misery, and prays for deliverance and a return to the happiness which was his in the past."[61]

In Psalm 51, the psalmist "humbly confesses his sins, begs for pardon and for restoration to God's favour, and promises thanksgiving."[62]

In Psalm 61, the king, "mindful of God's protection in the past, appeals to Him for aid, and promises thanksgiving when the crisis is past . . ."[63]

The sixth section contains Psalms 63, 67, 71, and 74.

Psalm 63 expresses a yearning for God, because the psalmist is confident that God will deliver the person from his or her enemies and from any troubles.[64]

---

58. Kissane, *The Book of Psalms,* I, 168.

59. Kissane, *The Book of Psalms,* I, 176.

60. Kissane, *The Book of Psalms,* I, 181.

61. Kissane, *The Book of Psalms,* I, p. 185.

62. Kissane, *The Book of Psalms,* I, 224.

63. Kissane, *The Book of Psalms,* I, 261.

64. Kissane, *The Book of Psalms,* I. 267.

The background to Psalm 67 is that:

> God has given a fruitful harvest, and the psalmist takes occasion to pray that through His goodness thus shown towards His people, the gentiles may be brought to honour Him as the true God.[65]

Psalm 71 is a hope for deliverance from trouble, with a promise of thanksgiving upon experiencing salvation.[66] Psalm 74 is a psalm describing a disaster that has befallen Israel. The psalmist prays for deliverance from the enemy.[67]

The seventh section contains Psalms 85, 86, 91, and 102.

In Psalm 85, the writer

> puts his message of hope in the form of a divine revelation; better times at hand; the fidelity of Israel will be rewarded and God will grant prosperity and happiness.[68]

In Psalm 86, because God is forgiving and merciful, it says here that God will save the faithful from trouble.[69]

In Psalm 91, the just one knows he or she will be saved, because

> the sinner will meet with trouble and sorrow during his life and will die prematurely. The just man will be saved from peril of premature death, and in the normal troubles of life he will be under God's care.[70]

In Psalm 102,

> a lamentation is expressed by an exile stricken with a fatal disease, who feels that he will not survive to see the restoration of Sion. His only consoling thought is that

---

65. Kissane, *The Book of Psalms*, I, 285.

66. Kissane, *The Book of Psalms*, I, 308.

67. Kissane, *The Book of Psalms*, II, 9.

68. Kissane, *The Book of Psalms*, II, 73.

69. Kissane, *The Book of Psalms*, II, 76.

70. Kissane, *The Book of Psalms*, II, 106.

God, being eternal, will in due time bring about the fulfillment of His promise . . .[71]

The final and eighth section is composed of Psalms 103, 104, 115, and 118.

Psalm 103 is a hymn of thanksgiving to God for God's dealings with mercy and goodness towards Israel.[72]

God is the creator of the universe and of all living things, and all God's creatures both on land and in the sea depend upon God for their continued existence.[73]

Psalm 115 is a:

> prayer for deliverance and at the same time a message of hope to the people Israel in a time of national humiliation.[74]

Psalm 118 is also a song of rejoicing in God's deeds.[75]

These psalms set the tone for their respective sections/*sedarim*. It has been shown that these psalms, and the verses from *Tanach* that are quoted with them, are appeals to God's mercy and goodness to save one from trouble and death. The psalmist asks God to forgive any sins and promises that praise and thanksgiving will be forthcoming upon salvation.

The appeal to God's mercy in these sections is referred to in the instruction written before the thirteen psalms, which conclude this section of *sedarim*:

> More so psalms 128, 130, 134, 139, 140, 141, 142, 148, 149, and 150 are worthy to petition mercy in accordance with the intention of these eight sedarim.[76]

This instruction also mentions that the reader does not have to say all thirteen of these psalms, because there is no fixed halacha

71. Kissane, *The Book of Psalms*, II, 141.

72. Kissane, *The Book of Psalms*, II, 147.

73. Kissane, *The Book of Psalms*, II, 151.

74. Kissane, *The Book of Psalms*, II, 206.

75. Kissane, *The Book of Psalms*, II, 216.

76. Berechiah, *Maavor*, 84.

for this ritual. This points to the non-halachic, unfixed, nature of many of these rituals for the sick. There has never been an analysis, to my knowledge, of the origin of the rituals and their accompanying prayers found in *Maavor Yabok*. An analysis of these thirteen psalms reveals that they continue these themes of God's mercy and judgement.

Whereas it was suggested in the text of *Maavor Yabok*[77] that these *sedarim* just discussed, which are composed of verses from the *Tanach*, should be said by the sick person in conjunction with the visitor, the rubric after the *sedarim* states that it is

> good for the sick one to accustom himself to saying the chapters of Our Teacher Saadia Gaon's prayer which is written in our work 'Awakeners of the Dawn' in the seder of the fourth, fifth, and sixth day.[78]

The following prayer of Saadia Gaon is based on the sick person's desire to request mercy from his or her creator.[79] This appeal to God's mercy is emphasized.

This prayer begins in an unusual way. Rather than the prayer's basis of appeal being to God's mercy upon a person's humble and sinful nature (as will be seen subsequently, this is a main characteristic of the confession and petitionary prayers), the prayer commences with a declaration of the petitioner's righteousness: "I in righteousness will behold Your face and will be satisfied in the awakening of Your vision."[80] The petitioner also says to God that he or she does not want to die, because work and life are not yet completed. The person says: "That I know myself that I have not had sufficient time to complete my work that You have sent me to do."[81]

These statements in Saadia's prayer are interesting because they question the inopportune moment of death's arrival. They

77. Berechiah, *Maavor,* 55.
78. Berechiah, *Maavor,* 88.
79. Berechiah, *Maavor,* 88.
80. Berechiah, *Maavor,* 23b.
81. Berechiah, *Maavor,* 23b.

go against the religious ideal of the "acceptance of sufferings," in which death is also viewed as a "suffering" that then is seen as an offering for expiation of one's committed sins. This runs counter to the rabbinic teaching found in R. Akiba's famous dictum, "Receive sufferings from love." The acceptance of sufferings, as was discussed earlier, does not mean resignation. Rather, it becomes a strategy on the road to repentance, which can be used to overcome sickness as well as death.

Beginning with the second paragraph of this prayer, its author admits of his sins, and prays that repentance will be an atonement for sins committed. This atonement will bring on healing of the disease that has afflicted the person: "And receive me in perfect repentance and help me to do good in Thy eyes."[82]

Because the middle section of this prayer calls for the recital of a confession of sin, it can be seen as an act of repentance bringing the repentant one back into a relationship with God. The similarity of this theme of a "renewed relationship" with God echoes the themes stressed in the psalms quoted in the eight sections:

> Place in me proper advice in order that all my deeds, and all my statements, and all my thoughts will be directed toward service of You, and You will forgive all I have transgressed. . . . Increase Your strength and power to destroy and restrain all that rises against me and to destroy the troubles of my soul.[83]

It is then suggested after three prayers (which three prayers are not specified) a confession is said, in the same way the confession is said on Yom Kippur.[84] The prayer of confession is an act of repentance and thus is also an act of "renewed relationship" with God. As such, it, too, echoes the psalms. As discovered earlier, the act of repentance that follows an acceptance of the reality of one's sickness and/or death is a strategy to fight sickness and death used both on the day of death and on Yom Kippur.

82. Berechiah, *Maavor,* 24a.
83. Berechiah, *Maavor,* 24b.
84. Berechiah, *Maavor,* 88.

As a final part to this opening section, it is suggested that the prayer found in the fourth part of *Maavor Yabok*, entitled "Entreaty of the Cloud of Incense," is to be read. It is stated that this prayer was arranged by Berechiah's teacher from Mantua.[85]

This prayer is based on the idea that just as offerings of incense were once offered as an atonement for sins, with the destruction of the Temple, praying the biblical verses that mention such offerings was a substitution for the actual offerings. The prayer begins with a quotation of the story concerning the cakes that Abraham asked Sarah to prepare for the three angels who appeared as men at Sodom. There is also the story of Israel's command to his sons regarding what incense and spice they should take to Joseph in Egypt. These two references set the tone here as one of a propitiatory effect. The worshipper wants to propitiate God with these offerings of incense, which the worshipper can no longer perform after the destruction of the Temple in Jerusalem. Therefore, there is a reading that substitutes for the act of offering the incense.

Propitiation thus becomes another strategy for influencing the Divine decree. This is done by reading the appropriate verses that mention offerings. Propitiation is also positively affected by considering one's sickness or death as an atonement offering (this will be explained subsequently).

The second paragraph mentions the incense offerings offered by the priest Aaron as atonement for sins.

The third paragraph mentions the proper proportions of ingredients that composed the incense offerings.

The fourth paragraph contains a prayer for health:

> as we have no priest, no fire-pan, no coals, no altar, no incense, and naught remains for us but the conversation of our lips as it is said: 'so we will render as bullocks the words of our lips.' it be Your will O Adonai our God and God of our Ancestors that our words be received before the seat of Your glory, as if we brought before You incense and You will hold back the plague.[86]

85. Berechiah, *Maavor, rpt,* 334.

86. Berechiah, *Maavor, rpt,* 334.

The mystical intent of this prayer asks for special concentration on the specific words describing the kinds of incense.[87] Whereas *Sefer HaHayiim* quotes R. Isaac as saying that the study of biblical portions, which discuss the laws and ceremonies of sin and guilt offerings, accomplishes the same effect as if those sacrifices had been brought, *Sefer HaHayiim* does not have one specific group of prayers devoted to the offerings. Therefore, it does not put to work the efficaciousness of the sacrifice passages. It also does not stress the importance of concentrating on specific words, as does *Maavor Yabok*, which is a necessary part of the Kabbalist's process of prayer.

In summary of these two texts, there is a great similarity in their focus. Both *Maavor Yabok* and *Sefer HaHayiim* are representative of the genre of literature in the tradition of a *Chevra Kadisha* manual. In this first section, both texts are laying the groundwork for the various rituals and prayers to be offered by both the ill person and those visiting him or her from the community. For the most part, these texts, however, differ in the specifics of not so much what to do but how a person offers these prayers and conducts these rituals. *Sefer HaHayiim* presents the rituals and prayers, while *Maavor Yabok* also describes how they function in the hands of one who knows their kabbalistic metaphysical underpinnings. This knowledge adds a spiritual effect to the offered rituals and prayers.

Maavor Yabok relies heavily upon the kabbalistic teachings that Berechiah received from his teachers in Italy. He is able to bring the reciter of these prayers and the practitioners of these rituals to a state of inner awareness as to the spiritual power and benefit of these practices from the tradition. *Sefer HaHayiim*, on the other hand, relates the traditional prayers and rituals with little reaching into the spiritual benefits or opportunities available through them to their practitioner. Frankfurter's work stands firmly in the rabbinic tradition which simply states the purpose of doing these things for the sick and how to do them. Because of the traditional sources each author finds for his material, Berechiah's work seems

87. Berechiah, *Maavor, rpt,* 333.

to stress God's mercy before judgement, while Frankfurter takes the opposite approach. For both authors, however, neither mercy nor judgment is offered at the exclusion of the other because both are a *definite* part of Judaism's God-human dynamic relationship.

These differences and similarity will become evident as this analysis of these texts continues.

Chapter IV

Prayers and Rituals for the Sick

AFTER THE INITIAL INTRODUCTORY readings and prayers, both *Sefer HaHayiim* and *Maavor Yabok* begin with prayers said upon entering a sick person's room. From this point on, the prayers found in both books follow the chronological order of the process from sickness to death.

Sefer HaHayiim

Sefer HaHayiim says that upon entering the room of the sick, these verses should be said:

> 'And the Eternal will take away from thee all sickness, and will put none of the evil diseases of Egypt, which you know, upon you but will lay them upon all those who hate you.' And God said: 'If you will diligently hearken unto the voice of the Eternal your God, and will do that which is right in God's sight, and will give ear to God's commandments, and keep all of God's statues, then I will put none of these diseases upon you which I have brought upon the Egyptians; for I am the Eternal who heals you.' 'I create the fruit of the lips; peace, peace, to

him that is far off, and to him that is near, says the Eternal, and I will heal him.'[1]

In the introduction to these verses, the author reveals why these were chosen. Using the method of gematria, he points out that the fifty-four words of these verses are equivalent to the numerical value of the letters in the Hebrew phrase "That I will live." It is implied that the efficacious influence of these verses arises from the numerical connection between the number of words and the phrase "That I will live," which verbalizes the hopes of the sick one.

The kabbalistic plays on numbers, phrases, and words are within parentheses in this edition of *Sefer HaHayiim*. Moreover, what is in parentheses contains a unique style and mode of interpretation as well as a distinctive style of writing compared with what is outside the parentheses. From the text itself, it is not possible to determine if the kabbalistic additions in *Sefer HaHayiim* were placed there by Frankfurter or by someone else.

As to the prayer's thematic content, it speaks of God's justice more than God's mercy. It emphasizes God's justice, because the first two verses point out the one-to-one quality of man's actions in relation to God's actions. If a person follows God's ways, God will not give that person the diseases of the Egyptians. The third verse also affirms this relationship between actions as sin and illness.

Although the revelation of its numerical meaning using the method of gematria points to a kabbalistic source, interestingly it was used by the author of *Sefer HaHayiim* but not by the author of *Maavor Yabok*, because the latter does not include this prayer. This same prayer is found in *Tozeoth Chaiim*, a liturgical handbook that was published in Roedelheim, Germany, in 1871.

Maavor Yabok

Maavor Yabok has the visitor reciting a different prayer upon confronting a person who is ill. The instructions included with this

1. Ascher, *The Book of Life*, 105.

prayer ask the visitor to say these words to petition mercy upon the sick one. This goal of the visit (that is, a petition for mercy upon the sick person) has since become *Halacha*, Jewish law and practice. The halachic statement found in the *Shulhan Aruch* is:

> As he requests mercy upon him, he will petition in any language he wishes ... he will be included among the sick of Israel and he will say: 'May God have mercy upon you among the sick of Israel.'[2]

The prayer in *Maavor Yabok* is:

> May no evil approach you, nor any plague come near your tent, that God's angels God will cause to watch over you in all your ways. Heal us O Adonai and we shall be healed, save us O Adonai and we shall be saved, as You are our praise.[3]

Berechiah goes on to explain this prayer. The evil is illness, and it is God's angels who watch over a person's ways. In describing the influence of this prayer upon the *Sefirot* Berechiah writes, quoting from the *Zohar*:

> As they are with the person, the Shechinah is found there to watch you in all your ways, that the ways are from Malchut to Tiferet, from Tiferet to Malchut by way of Yesod ... as is mentioned above. And he will concentrate on the powers which pour forth from the King on High to heal all the flesh which are deposited in the palaces above. And also, God will have in mind, by his saying, 'that God's angels God will command unto you,' channels of lights that are appointed over the departing soul so that the soul will not be troubled in its departure, that God-forbid, death be decreed upon it. And it is written in סבא אליהו p.98b that the Holy One Praised be He walks on wings of wind to bring healing to the world. It is Raphael who is influenced by Malchut, who

---

2. Caro, *Shulhan Aruch, Yoreh Deah*, 3, 167a.
3. Berechiah, *Maavor*, 88.

receives from Tiferet, that places healing by strength by the crown on high.[4]

The kabbalistic system is seen at work in this quotation. This prayer sets into motion the *Sefirot* and the angel Raphael. It describes the strategy of prayer, but also analyzes and specifies the process. Such an analysis is not to be found in *Sefer HaHayiim*. The prayer also gives some psychological insight by saying that by the presence of angels "the soul will not be troubled in its departure. . . ." Knowledge of the presence of these angels would give great comfort to the sick. By theosophical knowledge of how this prayer influences the Divine, the dying person derives psychological and spiritual comfort by knowing of God's protection.

The word רפאינו (rephaeinu) that appears in this prayer is also analyzed kabblistically; that is, in reference to the *Sefirot*. The first three letters, *resh, pay,* and *aleph,* are drawn to the sphere Kindness (Hesed):

> And the crown does not influence the sefirot but by Hesed. And ne-ra-phay is below by Tiferet and Malchut. The nun and vav are the foundation of the souls of Israel, which grasp Tiferet, foundation of vav and Malchut, foundation of nun, which are necessary for healing . . .[5]

At this point in the liturgy of *Maavor Yabok*, it is suggested that one concentrate on the intention of visiting the sick. Berechiah is developing here a mindfulness for the fulfillment of this mitzvah. He first quotes from the Talmud the idea that the person who visits the sick takes on 1/60th of the sick one's illness.[6]

Then, in the language and idea system of the Kabbalah, he writes:

> And thus the man who is to be engaged in this mitzvah causes to pour forth from above power and strength, as he strengthens the sick one by his visit, and lightens the strength of the evil over the sick one as mentioned . . .

4. *Berechiah, Maavor,* 48.

5. *Berechiah, Maavor,* 48.

6. *Talmud Baba Metzia,* 30.

and he who visits the sick is from the side of the attribute of Kindness, and with his engagement with his healing, he ascends until the three sefirot that from there he draws strength and healing . . .[7]

Maavor Yabok and *Sefer HaHayiim*

It is interesting how *Maavor Yabok*, as a liturgical handbook as well as a handbook on customs, interweaves theosophy with already established Jewish customs. This gives theological and theosophical knowledge to the practical fulfillment of various mitzvot pertaining to the acts of kindness. *Sefer HaHayiim* discusses visiting the sick from another viewpoint. Although it is acknowledged that prayer by the visitor is an important part of visiting,

> Rabbi Simon, son of Yochai, says: What is the actual duty of those who visit the sick? Are they only to be solicitous for the restoration of the bodily health of the sick? No, their chief object must be to provide the sufferers with spiritual remedy . . . awaken in the heart of the sick thoughts of piety . . .[8]

more than the efficacy of prayer is not enumerated, as it is understood as operative for the person who is ill.

> The efficacy of prayer performed by the righteous and those who devote their life to the study of the Divine Law, is practically borne out by numerous instances . . .[9]

The visitor, it is stated, helps the sick one both physically and monetarily, if necessary. He speaks words of "comfort and consolation."[10] The result of visiting, therefore, is described in *Sefer HaHayiim* in terms of the visitor.

---

7. Berechiah, *Maavor*, 214–215.
8. Ascher, *The Book of Life*, 1.
9. Ascher, *The Book of Life*, 77.
10. Ascher, *The Book of Life*, 71.

In *Maavor Yabok*, visiting the sick was described in terms of the visited, but also of the Divine world. *Sefer HaHayiim* sees visiting in terms of a religious duty. *Maavor Yabok* sees it also in terms of theosophical knowledge and influence. *Sefer HaHayiim*, in describing the rewards of the visited, also describes the rewards of visiting as gained by the visitor: "Rabbi Judah teacheth in the name of Samuel, he who visits the sick will escape the judgment of Gehinom . . ."[11]

This reward and punishment system even operative for the visitor is uppermost in the mind of *Sefer HaHayiim's* author:

> Rabbi Hannah Saba teaches, in the name of Rava: He who is able to pray for his fellow-men, i.e., who understands the nature of prayer, and neglects to perform it, is called a sinner . . . God is greatly pleased with the prayer offered to him on behalf of the sick. The Ramban terms these prayers, 'seeking of God' . . .[12]

Maavor Yabok also has a special prayer to be said by the visitor only upon visiting a 'Master of Torah,' or one who is learned:

> May it be God's will, that he will be blessed from the mouth of the Holy One Praised be He and His Shechinah with each of God's attributes, and God's ten sephirot, with all God's names, and from the four supports, and the six steps of the throne and from all the heads of the Yeshiva above, and from all of the angels and from all the family above and the family below in a short and quick time. And may a healing be accounted to you, and may God heal you from your stripes, and from the light of God, the ancient one, may God quickly bring unto you salvation. And may God, by God's great and merciful name, be merciful to you with all the sick of Israel who are in need of mercy, Amen. Selah. May the words of my mouth and the meditations of my heart be acceptable unto You, O Adonai, my rock, and my redeemer.[13]

---

11. Ascher, *The Book of Life*, 65.

12. Ascher, *The Book of Life*, 69.

13. Berechiah, *Maavor*, 88–89.

It is evident how this prayer calls upon all the sources of power available to the mystic, as well as to the person who is sick, which are the Divine Presence, God's attributes of mercy and healing, the *Sefirot*, God's names, God's throne, the angels, and God's family. Notice, that this prayer is only offered for one who is knowledgeable in this kabbalistic imagery. The goal of this is to bring on healing through God's mercy. The request is not for the mere cessation of pain or an easy death, but for a real cure.

Chapter V

THE CONFESSION OF SIN—THE *VIDUI*

AFTER THE PRAYERS TO be said upon entering the room of the sick person, *Maavor Yabok* moves into the confession of sins, while *Sefer HaHayiim* first has a number of prayers said as an introduction to the prayers of confession. Such a difference between the two texts could be attributed more to the available liturgies circulated in their respective areas, northern versus southern Europe, than to the stress the texts placed upon the confessional liturgy.

Sefer HaHayiim

The first prayer in *Sefer HaHayiim* in the introduction to the confessions, which can be called "A Prayer of the Afflicted" from the first verse of the prayer, is read when one feels ill, or his wife or children feel ill, or when he suffers from a pecuniary loss. Notice should be taken that this prayer, which is included in a book of prayers and customs for the sick and dying, is read at the time of any loss, and not just at the loss of health. The one who suffers a loss should pray this prayer immediately as the judgment of heaven is upon him. This person is to analyze his or her deeds, and to say to the angel: "Your hand be weakened."[1]

---

1. Ascher, *The Book of Life*, 106.

48

It is also written,

> Nothing happens by accident, but rather by the provi-
> dence of the Holy One Praised be He who is exacting with
> His righteous as a hairsbreadth, as it is written: 'it shall be
> very tempestuous round about him', to bring upon him
> 'the disease which I placed upon the Egyptians I will not
> place upon you', that 'I am the Lord your healer.'[2]

This comment certainly shows God to be an executor of ex-
acting justice with God's righteous people. The sick one must look
through his or her deeds to find out why they are being punished,
because it is believed that there is a direct relationship between
sin and sickness. This relationship between sin and sickness begins
to point toward the soon to be offered confessional prayer. This
relationship also echoes the relationship between sickness and sin
as seen by the rabbis, which was described earlier in Chapter II.

It is interesting that part of this comment regarding sin and
sickness is in parentheses and is written in a unique style from
what is written outside the parentheses, as was seen earlier. This
inner comment again uses the vocabulary and mode of interpreta-
tion of the Kabbalist.

The tone of the material within the parentheses is immediate-
ly recognized as different from what surrounds it, because mercy
is now stressed over judgment, as seen in the following quotations:

> The 54 verses of the petition of mercy reverse the at-
> tribute of judgment to mercy. To fix the breach in the
> name of הוי"ה that is mercy as ה"י וי"ו יו"ד ה"י which is
> equivalent to חסד and by his sin's judgment comes upon
> him by the name אדונות. [3]

> It happens that the numerical equivalent of the name
> אדונות and דן, judge, is 54 which is equivalent to the
> numerical value of God's name יו"ד ה"א וי"ו ה"א. The
> judgment, punishment for sin, functions then as an in-
> centive to do repentance which returns the letters יו"ד

2. Ascher, *The Book of Life*, 106.

3. Ascher, *The Book of Life*, 106.

ה״י וי״ו וי״ד to א״ה וי״ו ה״א and thereby brings on mercy (*Hesed*).[4]

Punishment thus functions to awaken the person to overcome the evil inclination, to do repentance. This repentance influences the divine harmony in the *Sefirot* and their system, which seeks homeostasis. The result of both explanations, the explanations inside and outside the parentheses, is to bring the sick one to the act of repentance.

However, the means and the knowledge to either be healed or face death differ between the two explanations found in this text. The explanation outside the parentheses describes God's judgment and exacting justice. Healing is brought as a reward for the sick one's repentance, which then depends upon God's mercy. This explanation describes what happens between a person and God, but it contains no theosophical knowledge as to how this process of healing comes about. This explanation, which can be viewed as reflecting a rabbinic attitude toward a person's relationship with God, seems to see justice as God's overriding mechanism in dealing with humanity. Mercy comes into play after justice has been exacted.

The explanation within the parentheses, however, presents a theosophical knowledge of this healing process. It differs in that it sees mercy, not justice, as God's overriding mechanism in dealing with humanity. It therefore reflects the kabbalah's system of the hierarchy and mechanism of the *Sefirot*. The explanation states that sin has disturbed the harmony of the *Sefirot* and God's attribute of mercy. By repentance, the harmony is returned as the letters of God's name are changed to their proper order. When this occurs the divine attribute of judgment moves back to mercy.

These differences between the two explanations seems more a difference in terminology than anything else. While one has a knowledge of the process and the other can only describe it, one seeing a different overriding mechanism than the other, the underlying process of both explanations is the same. This process is the

4. Ascher, *The Book of Life*, 106.

rabbinic idea, as described earlier, that God reacts to the person's needs. Regardless of why or how God does this, it is this underlying process that makes repentance, and therefore healing, possible. In the prayer itself, the sick person pours out his or her heart to God, asking God not to turn away from the person offering this petitionary prayer. The person sees God as his or her shield and glory, who will answer when called upon.

After this introduction, there is an appeal to God's mercy by praying, "O Eternal, rebuke me not in Thine anger, nor chastise me in Thy wrath. Have mercy upon me, O Eternal!"[5] The person asks God to blot out the transgressions committed from youthful years. There is a petition asking God to take this into consideration. There is the recognition that God is the ruling power over all. There is the hope that by turning to God again, there will be healing.

> Trust ye in the Eternal forever; for in the eternal God is everlasting strength. The Eternal will give strength unto His people, the Eternal will bless His people with peace. O God of Hosts, blessed is the man who trusteth in Thee. Save us, Eternal. May the King hear us when we call.[6]

The second part of this prayer appeals to God's exacting justice.

This sense of God's justice and therefore an acceptance of God's judgments is an essential part of the sick person's relationship with God.

> Sovereign of the universe, I know that just is Thy judgment; Thou hast tried me, but, alas! I was not found pure and guiltless. There was nothing to shield me against Thy sentence.[7]

Then, as the sick person recognizes his or her sins, a sense of humility comes on, an embarrassment about these sins, and again the one who is ill petitions:

5. Ascher, *The Book of Life*, 109.
6. Ascher, *The Book of Life*, 111.
7. Ascher, *The Book of Life*, 111.

> And Thou, merciful God, look down upon my trouble,
> and count it to me as an atonement. I beseech Thee to
> spare me, and all the members of my household. Om-
> nipotent ruler! Terminate my trouble and sufferings and
> change the evil decree for my good.[8]

The third section of this prayer, רחם (*racheim*), appeals to
God's mercy and kindness. As God will have compassion, the sick
one, when this person is healed, will praise God, and tell of God's
wonders.

The fourth section, אתה הראת, begins with an acknowledg-
ment of God's justice which the sick one hopes will be tempered
with mercy.

> O mayest Thou, in Thine infinite mercy, support me,
> and grant pardon for all my transgressions against Thee,
> for which Thou hast visited me with Thy chastisements.
> I know that Thy judgments are right, but merciful and
> gracious art Thou . . .[9]

Notice that this prayer expresses the rabbinic idea that God's
strict justice must be tempered with mercy. The paragraphs of this
prayer therefore alternate between judgment and mercy.

The teaching is then offered that even God's chastisements
are for a person's good. As seen earlier, the strategy of acceptance
of God's deeds is made a part of the liturgical texts. This ability to
change the decree of God through repentance, acceptance of one's
sin, and then change is also a part of the Yom Kippur liturgy.

> Lo! all these things worketh God oftentimes forbear-
> ingly with man, to withdraw his soul from the pit, to be
> enlightened with the light of the living. For He (God)
> will not impose upon man more than right; to cite him
> before His mighty throne of judgment. . . . touching
> the Almighty, we cannot find Him out; He is excellent
> in power, and in judgment, and in plenty of justice . . .
> Behold! happy is the man whom God correcteth; there-
> fore, despise not thou the chastening of the Almighty:

8. Ascher, *The Book of Life*, 111.
9. Ascher, *The Book of Life*, 113.

For He maketh sore and bindeth up: He woundeth and
His hands heal . . .[10]

The fifth and sixth sections appeal to God's mercy to bring
on this healing. There is a recognition of God's power over life.
In quite realistic terms, original phrases and biblical phrases are
interwoven to express this hope:

> Deign that my pain and suffering may abate, like the
> visible decrease of the lunar light, whilst the health and
> vigour of my bodily frame may be renewed like unto the
> moon in her renewal; grant that my youthful strength
> may again be like that of the eagle.[11]

In this prayer from *Sefer HaHayiim*, no allusions are made
to kabbalistic doctrines or modes of interpretation. The underly-
ing idea is rabbinic in focus: that is, mercy is a check on God's
judgment, which is God's means for ruling the universe. Mercy is,
in a sense, a reward for accepting God's judgment. There are less
complete verses quoted here from the Bible than verses quoted in
Maavor Yabok. The latter seems to depend more heavily on biblical
verses than the former for the content of many of its prayers.

The next group of prayers in both *Maavor Yabok* and *Sefer
HaHayiim* comprise the ודוי (*vidui*), the confession. That this sec-
tion is the central section of these liturgies for the sick and dying
is demonstrated by its overall length. The confession in *Maavor
Yabok* is composed of three main parts with an introduction and
a conclusion. *Sefer HaHayiim* contains a general confession of sin,
and a confession for those on their deathbed.

---

10. Ascher, *The Book of Life,* 115.
11. Ascher, *The Book of Life,* 117.

Maavor Yabok

The importance of the confession is underscored in *Maavor Yabok* by its announcement:

> From all which has been said, we saw that every man needs to meditate and to articulate his sins before his king and in particular by the confession on the death-bed.[12]

And in *Sefer HaHayiim* the importance of the confession is stressed in the comment: "But if he repents even at the last moment of his life he will be saved . . ."[13]

The centrality and importance of the confession also has an historical basis. The Talmud, tractate *Semachot*, specifies two types of prayer: those said by the sick person and those for the sick person. And as mentioned before, the first prayer is a prayer for mercy; it is quite short and very general in content, because it is handed down from the Talmud and in the codes. The second prayer is the confession.

The prayer of the deathbed confession, as it appears in Talmud *Semachot* and in the *Shulhan Aruch, Yoreh Deah*, is:

> I confess before Thou, O Lord, my God and God of my Fathers, that my healing and my death are in Thy hand. May it be Thy will that Thou wilt heal me with a perfect healing, and that if I will die, may my death be an atonement for all my sins, iniquities, and transgressions which I have committed perversely before Thee. . . . And grant me a portion in the Garden of Eden, and cause me to merit the life in the world to come, which is reserved for the righteous.[14]

Realizing the brevity of this confession, the *Shulhan Aruch*, quoting from *Kol Bo*, says that the sick person can also say the Yom

---

12. Berechiah, *Maavor*, 140.
13. Ascher, *The Book of Life*, 44.
14. Karo, *Shulchan Aruch*, 168a.

Kippur liturgical confession.[15] Again, a connection is made between the Yom Kippur liturgy and the liturgy for the day of death.

The centrality and importance of this prayer of confession is also demonstrated by its appearance in Isaiah Horowitz's work, *Shnei Luehot Habrit*. This work was one of the major kabbalistic works pertaining to customs and practices in the 16th and 17th centuries.

The reason Horowitz devoted so much of this section to the confession, both its laws and prayers, is presented in many kabbalistic and rabbinic texts that he quotes. One text, which is from the *Zohar*, puts great weight upon the confession and its relation to the future health of the individual in this world and even in the next. Even in this comment to the prayer of confession, emphasis is placed on the visited and upon the visitor. It goes as far as to call the visitor an "angel of goodness." This importance of the ability of the visitor to urge the visited one to confess is seen in the quotation:

> In the Zohar, parashat Pekudai, 'he who watches the sick and attempts to get him to return in repentance, behold he is as the advocate of goodness, that he causes him to be saved from the attribute of stern judgment, and save him from death, and redeem him from destruction, and cause him revival of life . . . [16]

As was seen earlier, within its explanation on the confessional prayers, *Maavor Yabok* describes the kabbalistic theosophical system, the process of the various prayers and customs and how they are efficacious. As to why Berechiah includes three confessions in his liturgy, he writes:

> and the sick one will concentrate on uniting in his confession three confessions corresponding to sin, transgression, and iniquity, and to include the major and minor alphabets, and he will mend first by Binah, and second, Tiferet, and third Malchut, and to mend Tiferet,

---

15. Karo, *Shulchan Aruch*, 167a.
16. Horowitz, *Shnei Luehot Ha-Brit*, II, 4a.

Malchut, and Yesod which are breached by sin, trans-
gression, and iniquity.[17]

This comment offers that kabbalistic linkage between man
and the Divine, because the specific words of the confession and
the confession itself have a direct influence upon God, in this case
the *Sefirah* of Keter, the spiritually highest of the *Sefirot*. The act of
the confessional prayer, with its specific words and order, has the
ability to bring together the *Sefirot* of the middle pillar of Mercy,
which is *Tiferet* (the King), *Yesod* (the Foundation), and *Malchut*
(the Queen), thus bringing about harmony through the *Sefirot*, the
heavenly heights.

This process is not stated explicitly or implicitly in *Sefer
HaHayiim's* comment on repentance:

> But if he repents even at the last moment of his life, he
> will be saved, as Scripture says: If there be a messenger
> with him, an 'interpreter, one among a thousand to show
> unto man his uprightness, then He is gracious unto
> Him, and says: 'Deliver him from going down into the
> grave: I have found a ransom (Job XXXII. 24, 25). Yea,
> he will then escape death, the pangs of Gehinom, and
> attain future bliss. This happy change may be wrought by
> repentance. . . . And not only does repentance mend the
> sinner, but even ranks him amongst the righteous . . .[18]

Again, *Sefer HaHayiim* uses texts that speak in rabbinic and
therefore biblical terms of reward and punishment. These texts
do not display the theosophical knowledge of the Divine process
that the kabbalistic texts do, as quoted in *Maavor Yabok*; rather,
Sefer HaHayiim describes the actual practice of the ritual and not
a descriptive underpinning theosophically of how the ritual has a
cosmic or spiritual effect.

The text of *Maavor Yabok* suggests that before the full text
of the confession is read, the sick person should read the confes-
sion written by Nachmanides. The text of this confession is found

17. Berechiah, *Maavor*, 147–148.
18. Ascher, *The Book of Life*, 44–45.

The confession in *Maavor Yabok* begins with a reading of Psalm 4, which can be said to be a declaration by David to have faith and security in God even in the face of one's enemies. The two uses here of the verb "to lie down" make this psalm particularly applicable to the reader who also is lying down on his sickbed. These two uses of this verb are: "Tremble and sin not, speak in your heart upon your bed and be silent, selah . . ." and "I will both lie down and sleep in peace because Thou O Lord makest me dwell alone in safety."[22]

The first confession opens with a humbling of the self. The worshipper asks God not to deny his petitions, because he admits he is stiff-necked and a sinner. There is then a list of sins. As each sin is enumerated in a few words, it echoes the confession of sins in the Yom Kippur liturgy. More than just being a random listing of sins, though, it is an alphabetical list, because each letter of the alphabet starts two sins. The sins are not only ethical but also ritualistic and ceremonial in nature.

The first confession ends with the knowledge that although a person has turned aside from God's commandments, God is just and true. God has not turned aside from him, because God is *Emet*, which can be translated as "faithful"[23] and *Tzadik* as "one who is true."[24] Because God knows all hidden and revealed thoughts, the sick person appeals to God's mercy to forgive him for his sins and has the faith that this will happen.

The emphasis of this confession is on a person's lack of faithfulness, and thus on a reliance upon God's faithfulness in their relationship with one another. This puts the sick person in the active role, in that he or she, by these actions, can correct this broken relationship with God. The confessor asks God in God's mercy to know, both by revealed and hidden thoughts, the person's turning from sinful ways, that is, repentance.

The second confession is little more than an expansion of the confession found in *Talmud Semachot*. The invalid asks God if he

22. Berechiah, *Maavor*, 89–90.
23. Jastrow, *A Dictionary*, I, 793.
24. Jastrow, *A Dictionary*, II, 1263.

or she can be healed. If, however, this person must die, may his or her death be an atonement for all sins, so that this person can be worthy of entering the Garden of Eden with the other righteous people. This acceptance of death is partially a resignation to God's decree. It is also an active acceptance in that by accepting it, the death becomes an atonement that then makes this person worthy of various future rewards. Acceptance of death, as part of this confession, is a strategy for accepting and overcoming death.

This confession expands the Talmudic confession by asking that healing come because of the merit of King Hezekiah:

> May You aid me as You aided Hezekiah, King of Judah,
> during his illness . . .[25]

The story of King Hezekiah thus becomes a paradigm for this strategy of overcoming the decrees of God. The confession then asks God to deal with the sick one out of faithfulness and justice. "With an even hand You weigh me, and You will judge me, and by Your great light You will emblazon me."[26]

The third confession opens with an *Al Chayt* formula, reminiscent of the Yom Kippur liturgy. It first mentions those sins done intentionally and those conducted unintentionally, those made in secret and those performed in the open. It then lists the various parts of the body,

This *Al Chayt* formula is general in content. This list of sins is concluded by the following prayer for forgiveness, from the Yom Kippur liturgy: "And thus for what I caused to others, You will pardon, and forgive all . . ."[27] From this last statement in the confession, it would seem that these admitted sins are ethical in nature: that is, sins between persons.

There is then an appeal to God's mercy based on God's thirteen attributes as enumerated in Exodus 34:6–7. It is as if this biblical section of God's attributes is taken to stand as a witness to God's acts of mercy with a person:

25. Berechiah, *Maavor*, 91.
26. Berechiah, *Maavor*, 91.
27. Berechiah, *Maavor*, 92.

And by Your great mercies and by their strength which shine upon the earth and its inhabitants; by Your thirteen attributes which You have appointed over the gates of prayer, that they do not return empty . . .[28]

This appeal to God's mercy for forgiveness is continued by calling on God's name אהיה אשר אהיה (Eheyeh Asher Eheyeh) from which all mercy comes. It is hoped that God's mercy will forgive all the sick person's sins, for which he or she would be deserving of the punishments from heaven and those of the human court below.

The prayer enumerates the several types of punishments possible, and concludes this section of the confession by stating:

May it be Your will, Adonai, my God, and God of my Fathers, that by the merit of Abraham, Isaac, and Israel Your servants, that this confession will be acceptable before You. If I were stoned, I were burned, I were murdered, I were strangled according to Torah law in Your great court in Jerusalem because of the honor of Your great Name that I injured by the meditation or thought, word or deed, the first, second, third, or fourth letter of Your great, powerful, and awesome Name or by other such letters, or by other letters which are connected with them, then I have been deserving of these four deaths before Your throne of glory . . .[29]

These and all sins are thus destructions of God's names, and therefore God's mercy, and effect the harmony of the *Sefirot* that seek balance. The strategy of fixing this disharmony of the *Sefirot*, caused by sin, is to accept vicariously the various punishments of the heavenly and human courts. With this vicarious acceptance of punishment, harmony and mercy are returned. With this strategy in mind, the following it is written concerning one's death:

and may my soul depart in holiness and in purity upon the holiness of Your great name which revives all, and to appease each of its four letters. And may You, by Your

28. Berechiah, *Maavor*, 92.

29. Berechiah, *Maavor*, 93.

abundant mercy, return and unite upon me each of the
four letters from Your three essential names a הויה אהיה
אדנות, and may all of them emblazon together in the
worlds of Atzilut, Beriah, Yetzirah, and Assiyah . . . May
Your will go out from the Crown of Mercy along the way
of the paths of thought, and prepare for me Your great-
ness and Your might, and I will be proud in the eternity
Netzach of Your majesty and I will be established in Your
kingdom Malchut.[30]

Repentance, as described in the previous paragraph, brings
about a harmony and unity to the letters of God's names, the vari-
ous worlds, and throughout the ten *Sefirot*. The last sentence of
this confession is composed of plays on the names of the *Sefirot*.

It is then described in this confession that with this estab-
lished harmony in the *Sefirot*, waters of life will flow down the
middle pillar of the Tree of Life that contains the sefirotic arrange-
ment, purifying all impurities. These are the waters of God's mercy.

The sick person then prays for strength to do away with
the impurities of the Evil Inclination. He or she hopes that death
should not come until the purification of the soul is achieved. This
purification of the soul is accomplished by confession and repen-
tance. Such purification, according to at least this confession, is
also conducted by God's appointed angels, who will enlighten this
person in the secrets of the Torah. The influence of theosophy and
theurgy are again evident. The goal of such preparations and strat-
egies in reference to death is that:

> My neshamah will unite with Your Neshamah, and my
> nefesh will praise You, and also my ruach inside of me
> will early seek Your name and I will walk in the light of a
> pure soul before the menorah . . . and bring me up with
> endearment to the Good Place that it has no limit, and I
> will depart in great love, and the neshamah that You gave
> pure unto me will be bound up in the bonds of life.[31]

30. Berechiah, *Maavor*, 93–94.

31. Berechiah, *Maavor*, 94.

Using a wealth of kabbalistic imagery, this third confession in *Maavor Yabok*, gives a description of what might be defined as a state of purity of soul: that is, a "good death." Such a good death is accomplished by repentance, by which the soul will find eternal peace and rest in a unity with God and the spheres.

The prayer that contains the forty-two-letter name of God, *Ana BaKoach*, begins the concluding section to the confessional prayer in *Maavor Yabok*. This prayer continues the petition of God's mercy. Once again, allusions are made to the worthiness of the ancestors, and an appeal is made to God's thirteen attributes of mercy:

> May You give truth to Jacob and mercy to Abraham which You swore to our Fathers since days gone by, and God will concentrate on the thirteen attributes of the macro prosopon as expounded in *Sefer Pardes*.[32]

This prayer does not mention death or its possibility; rather, it mentions suffering and terrible sickness. It is hoped that through God's mercy, this person's sins would be dashed into the depths, and no punishment would come by suffering or illness.

It is then suggested that the sick person read Psalm 121, which, as it begins "I will lift up my eyes unto the mountains from whence my help comes,"[33] speaks of God's ever-present help and protection. The last verse of this psalm would be especially comforting at the time after such extensive confessions. It speaks of God's protection at birth and at death. As it stated: "Adonai will watch your going out and coming in from this time forth and forever."[34] God is, thus, with a person throughout that person's life as well as death.

This section of prayers of confession in *Maavor Yabok* concludes with a basic recapitulation of the prayer *Ana BaKoach*. The prayer *Mi El Camocha* is then recited asking God to constrain God's anger and deal with the sick one in mercy and faithfulness.

---

32. Berechiah, *Maavor*, 95.
33. Berechiah, *Maavor*, 91.
34. Berechiah, *Maavor*, 91.

It states that if there must be suffering, it should come out of God's justice (restrained power) and not out of God's wrath (unrestrained power). The traditional prayer for health is said, and the prayer concludes with a number of verses from the evening service "Before Going to Bed," which call upon God's salvation and protection.

However, this prayer does not just reiterate the previous one; the order of its first three verses has a kabbalistic meaning referring to the thirteen attributes of God:

> And afterward he will say thirteen attributes which will increase their usage; length of days and healing will be brought up before him from these three verses. 1. 'Who is as You' 2. 'forgives iniquity' 3. 'pardons transgressions' 4. 'For the remainder of God's inheritance' 5. 'God will not increase God's anger always' 6. 'but God desires mercy' 7. 'God will turn, God will be merciful to us' 8. 'God will conquer our sins' 9. 'God will throw all our sins into the depths of the sea' 10. 'God will give truth to Jacob' 11. 'mercy to Abraham' 12. 'As You swore to our Fathers' 13. 'from days of old.'[35]

It is then suggested that the sick person pray the prayer *El Melech*, and if that person is a "student of wisdom," the prayer *Otanu al Shemecha* should also be offered. These prayers are not printed in the text. The traditional prayers from the liturgy, *Adon Olam* and *Yigdal*, are recited. These are both medieval poems based on the model of the "Thirteen Articles of Faith" of Maimonides, whose importance was described; they can also be explained to the sick person by his or her visitors: "and they will explain to him, each of the thirteen principles if it is necessary."[36]

The importance of the "Thirteen Principles" relates to the Kabbalist's stress on wisdom and metaphysical knowledge as means of purifying the soul and achieving eternal life. What I find to be most intriguing is that Berechiah brings the visitor into this by suggesting that he present a teaching of the meaning behind

35. Berechiah, *Maavor*, 154.

36. Berechiah, *Maavor*, 96.

these philosophical principles. The visitor of the sick and dying is then not only a vehicle for prayer but also a vehicle for the enlightenment that is necessary to either deal with one's illness or face one's death.

Sefer HaHayiim

Sefer HaHayiim has two confessions. The first is a general confession which would not to be said by one on a deathbed.

The first paragraph of the first confession is similar in form to the first confessional section in *Maavor Yabok*, although it is shorter in length. They both begin with the same phrase: "My God, and God of my Fathers! May my prayers come before You and hide not Yourself from my supplications."[37]

As in *Maavor Yabok*, there is a confession of a person's sinful nature:

> I have sinned against You all my life long unto this day,
> for I have acted foolishly; I am ashamed and confused;
> my evil inclinations enticed me to rebellion.[38]

There is also a listing of sins, like the list in the Yom Kippur liturgy. As in *Maavor Yabok*, the sins are listed alphabetically. However, whereas *Maavor Yabok* lists two or more sins for each letter, *Sefer HaHayiim* lists only one under each letter. The type of sin that *Sefer HaHayiim* seems to be lacking might be called sins that are ritualistic in nature.

Two examples would be sufficient here to demonstrate these differences. Whereas for the first letter of the alphabet in both books list the sin אשמתי (*ashamti*), "I have sinned," *Maavor Yabok* adds אכלתי (*achalti*), "I ate, things which were forbidden and abominable."[39] Whereas for the eighth letter in both books there is the sin חמסתי (*hamasti*), "I destroyed," *Maavor Yabok* adds, חללתי (*helalti*), "I profaned, the name of the Lord in secret and in

---

37. Ascher, *The Book of Life*, 118.

38. Ascher, *The Book of Life* 119.

39. Berechiah, *Maavor*, 90.

open; I profaned the sabbaths and holidays."[40] *Maavor Yabok* lists ritualistic sins in many cases, but *Sefer HaHayiim* does not seem to mention them at all, only ethical and moral sins.

Moreover, unlike much of the confession in *Maavor Yabok*, *Sefer HaHayiim* in this opening first part of the confession section does not mention the word "mercy" or its synonyms in relation to God. Rather, it speaks of the acceptance of God's justice:

> but You are just concerning all that is come upon us, for You have dealt most truly, and I have done most wickedly.[41]

The actual body of this first confession in *Sefer HaHayiim* begins with the prayer מה אומר (*Ma Omeir*). The confession begins with a declaration that God has knowledge of both revealed and hidden thoughts of a person. From a purview of confessional prayers, this type of declaration is essential to such a prayer. By such a declaration, the confessor protects himself or herself, in that even if a certain sin is not uttered, the sinner knows that God is aware of it and therefore can forgive it. This opening paragraph is finally concluded with an appeal to God's mercy.

There are then three paragraphs in which sins are enumerated in the form of the *Al Chayt* liturgical formula. Although it is difficult to discern a difference in content between the first two paragraphs, there appears to be a structural difference. The first paragraph does not list ethical sins between persons, such as "stubbornness of heart," "incestuous lewdness," "deceiving my neighbor," and "despising my parents and teachers,"[42] as does the second paragraph. The first paragraph, however, makes a point of stating that these sins were conducted "voluntarily and involuntarily," "publicly or secretly, deliberately or deceitfully," "presumptuously or accidentally."[43]

---

40. Berechiah, *Maavor*. 90.

41. Ascher, *The Book of Life*, 121.

42. Ascher, *The Book of Life*, 121.

43. Ascher, *The Book of Life*, 121.

By stating various types of motivation in this way, the first paragraph also covers all aspects of the sinful deed.

The third paragraph is like the third confession in *Maavor Yabok*. The confessor asks God to pardon him or her for all sins needed to bring trespass offerings or be liable to incur the punishments by stripes, barrenness, or death.

Each paragraph is followed by the liturgical formula from Yom Kippur: "And for all of these, You God of Pardon! O pardon me! O forgive me! O grant me remission!" [44] This appeal to God's mercy is followed through in the closing paragraphs of this first confession prayer in *Sefer HaHayiim*.

There is then an interim prayer between the general confession and the one said by a person on his deathbed. This interim prayer describes the efficaciousness of prayer. Once again, *Sefer HaHayiim* presents a description of the result of prayer, not theosophically, rather practically. It is written:

> A truly religious and godly man will never suffer himself to be overtaken by death: he will always prepare for it by ardent prayer, and humble submission to the Will of God. Confession, my brother, and pious sister has never accelerated death. On the contrary, prayer and confession very often cause our days to be prolonged, and our sins to be forgiven. [45]

This prayer begins by extolling God's holiness, knowledge, and healing powers. In God's hands is the power to strengthen and to heal. In very real terms, the prayer then goes on to describe one's illness and its vicissitudes:

> for all my limbs are as heavy on me as lead, crushed and dislocated. My days are consumed like smoke, and my bones are burnt as a hearth; my heart is smitten and withered like grass. [46]

44. Ascher, *The Book of Life*, 123.
45. Ascher, *The Book of Life*, 125.
46. Ascher, *The Book of Life*, 125.

This is situation is the result of God's anger:

> For Thine arrows stick fast in me, and Thy hand presseth
> me sore, there is no soundness in my flesh because of
> Thine anger . . .[47]

which is brought on by the sick person's sins "because of my
sin! for mine iniquities are gone over my head."[48]

The prayer now turns to an appeal, first to God's presence,
and then to God's mercy:

> Mine eyes are ever towards God; for He shall pluck my
> feet out of the tent. Turn Thou unto me, and have mercy
> upon me, for I am desolate and afflicted. . . . Have mercy
> upon me, O Eternal God; consider my trouble, which I
> suffer by those who hate me; O lift me up from the gates
> of death.[49]

In giving a reason God should save this ill person from death,
the prayer quotes the words of the psalmist, which were mentioned
earlier in the *Sefer HaHayiim*:

> For in death there is no remembrance of Thee, in the
> grave who shall give Thee thanks? . . . I will praise Thee,
> that Thou hast afflicted me, and art become my salvation.
> The dead praise not the Eternal, neither any that go down
> in silence.[50]

Death is described here in *Sefer HaHayiim* in terms of one
being unable to praise God. This idea of death is biblical. Various
verses from the psalms are quoted to present this idea. As was
seen earlier, *Maavor Yabok* describes death in terms of cosmic
disharmony and a cessation of Divine Light pouring forth from
the brighter *Sefirot* in reaction to sin. Although the terminologies
differ, both books see a person's ability to repent through word and
deeds as a strategy to overcome death.

47. Ascher, *The Book of Life*, 123.
48. Ascher, *The Book of Life*, 127.
49. Ascher, *The Book of Life*, 127.
50. Ascher, *The Book of Life*, 129–131.

The Confession of Sin—The Vidui

The first confession on the deathbed begins with a slight expansion of the confession found in the *Shulhan Aruch* and the second confession, *Maavor Yabok*. The dying person acknowledges God's power over life and death, illness, and recovery. As such, he or she prays to God for recovery. If this is impossible, then death should be an atonement for any sins, so that this person may receive the rewards in the life to come.

The second paragraph of this confession is a petition for more years of life. It recognizes that God does not want the death of a sinner: rather, repentance, so that "he may live." [51] He therefore makes a confession of his sins. The ill person then hopes that, based on the merits of Hezekiah and David, he or she should be given a cure from illness and therefore receive a long life.

This paragraph concludes this deathbed confession section in *Sefer HaHayiim*. It is interesting that it is much shorter than the confessional section *Maavor Yabok*. It is also certainly devoid of the kabbalistic allusions found in the confessions of *Maavor Yabok*.

51. Ascher, *The Book of Life*, 131.

Chapter VI

<!-- divider -->

THE EXTREMELY ILL—
PRAYERS AND RITUALS

Sefer Hahayiim

THE SECTION THAT FOLLOWS the confessions in *Sefer HaHayiim* contains prayers said by visitors for the extremely ill person. This section is preceded by a comment that is divided into two parts.

The first part describes the need for the sick one, as he or she goes through the process of confession, to ask forgiveness from any person he or she might have offended or hurt by word or deed. The ill person is both a sinner before God and before people. This very social act of repentance has been discussed earlier because it also appears in the confessional section of *Maavor Yabok*. In *Maavor Yabok*, the act of repentance toward others was conducted by an act of charity, צדקה (*tzedakah*), whose sum was interpreted by its mystical numerical value.

The second part is in parentheses. As with the earlier comments from *Sefer HaHayiim*, which appeared in parentheses, this comment's content is kabbalistic. It gives an example of the Kabbalist's doctrine of transmigration of the soul. It describes what happens to the person who fails to make monetary amends to those with whom he is in debt. This person put himself under the pain of transmigration, גלגול (*gilgul*). This is one of the few direct mentions of transmigration, which is reincarnation, in either book.

This comment is kabbalistic in content and noted by the comment by the preceding words: "And the wise men of Kabbalah wrote . . ." which would verify its source.[1]

As this discussion precedes the prayers by the visitor, *Sefer HaHayiim* quotes Rabbi Eleazar's statement on the prayer of the righteous and its influence. He states: ". . . the prayer of the righteous turns the Holy One Praised be He's attribute of anger to mercy."[2] The use of the term "attribute of anger" רגזנות (*ragzanut*) is noteworthy. Is Rabbi Eleazar equating God's attribute of anger with the more commonly used term God's "attribute of judgment"?

This section of prayers for the extremely ill is to be said by a minimum of ten visitors, which also indicates the spiritual power and comfort that comes from the presence of community. This is one of the few times that the presence of a minyan, 10 men in prayer, was mentioned. This prayer begins with a petition for permission from the Holy One Praised be He and God's Divine Presence.

The first paragraph is an Aramaic prayer that entreats God's mercy by quoting the thirteen attributes of God from Exodus 24:6. This prayer is also found in the Ari's siddur of the 18th century and in the Southern French work of the late 14th century *Orchoth Chayiim* by R. Aharon Hakohen Lunel. The latter work would seem to be the earliest mention of this prayer. Its bastardized Aramaic, which implies that it is not of zoharic origin, and its appearance in this early Sephardic work, might reflect an unfixed oral liturgy used by some of the early Sephardic Kabbalistic groups. Regarding this prayer, it is stated in *Orchoth Chayiim*: "And there are places that begin 'We pray and entreat' etc., and all follow after the custom: 'The Lord, Lord, God is merciful and gracious,' etc."[3]

1. Ascher, *The Book of Life*, 132.
2. Ascher, *The Book of Life*, 133.
3. Ha-Cohen from Lunel, *Orchot Chajim*, 559.

This first paragraph is followed by paragraphs in Hebrew that leave space to insert the sick person's name. This is one of the few instances in both books where the prayer is personalized. The rest of the prayer continues this appeal to God's mercy. Divine justice and judgment are not mentioned. Psalm 93 is then inserted. This is a psalm appealing to God's protection, but this protection comes out of justice rather than mercy.

This protection arises from God's overriding justice, because it is contingent on a person's deeds: "Because he delighteth in Me will I deliver him; I will exalt him because he hath known My name. When he calleth upon Me I will answer him . . ."[4] God's unmerited mercy is also mentioned here: "Like as a father pitieth his children, so the Eternal pitieth them that fear Him."[5]

This unmerited mercy is then colored by justice, that is, merited mercy, in the paragraph that begins:

> And He said, if thou wilt diligently hearken unto the voice of the Lord Eternal Thy God, and wilt do that which is right in His sight . . . I will put none of those diseases upon thee which I have brought upon the Egyptians . . .[6]

The idea that God's mercy is contingent on a person's repentance, and thereby tempered with justice, continues through the rest of the prayer: "The Eternal is good unto them that wait for God; to the soul that seek God."[7]

This intermingling of mercy and justice arises from the fact that these paragraphs are composed of biblical verses. As is the case with many of the psalms, they often balance the attributes of mercy and justice.

There is also a second group of prayers said for the extremely ill person by his visitors. In the first paragraph of this section, the visitors are depicted as officers bringing the prisoner to the scaffold. The image of God as stern judge is quite strong here:

4. Ascher, *The Book of Life*, 133.
5. Ascher, *The Book of Life*, 135.
6. Ascher, *The Book of Life*, 139.
7. Ascher, *The Book of Life*, 141.

> O Lord, God of Israel, hearken to the prayer and petition
> which Thy servants pray before Thee, forgive the sick one
> who is stretched on his bed as if they brought him up to
> the gallows to be judged . . .[8]

The reality of one's illness and suffering are vividly depicted when it says:

> He _____ the bittered soul; that all his couch is turned
> by his illness, he does not stand from it, his taste and
> smell are bittered, his soul will despise all food and the
> warmth of his inner heart touches the gates of death . . .[9]

After this description of the invalid's sickness, the visitor prays for healing from God by appealing to God's mercy. What has been termed merited and unmerited mercy both appear here. An example of an appeal to unmerited mercy would be:

> O Lord, be gracious unto him, heal his soul and forgive
> him because he has sinned against Thee.[10]

This is an unmerited act on God's part: it is because a person is sinful in nature, and not because of any act of repentance. God should be merciful and heal this sinner only because of a person's finite and weak nature.

An example of an appeal to merited mercy in this section would be: "The eye of the Lord is to those who fear Him, to those who wait for His kindness. "[11] Here, God's mercy is predicated upon a person's turning toward God in repentance, based on that person's fear of God.

Although this prayer repeatedly appeals to both mercy and justice, it recognizes a hierarchy between the two. This hierarchy is pointed out in the words:

---

8. Ascher, *The Book of Life*, 142.
9. Ascher, *The Book of Life*, 142.
10. Ascher, *The Book of Life*, 142.
11. Ascher, *The Book of Life*, 143

> And because of them He will remember, He will requite,
> be merciful, be forgiving, will save, will help, will protect,
> will save, and will heal _____ from all his illness.[12]

The verb "to requite" (פקד, *pakhad*) implies the exacting of judgment, and it is this act which precedes the act of mercy in the quotation. It was demonstrated earlier and will be seen subsequently in the section found in *Maavor Yabok*, which is equivalent to this section under discussion from *Sefer HaHayiim* (that is, prayers said for the extremely ill), that the former sees God's requiting of sin as before God's act of mercy more pervasively than the latter work. *Maavor Yabok* tends to see mercy, and not justice, as the overriding principle.

The concluding paragraphs of this section, then, emphasize an appeal to God's mercy. There can be little doubt that these prayers were from a Kabbalistic tradition. The prayer printed here[13] that asks that the twenty-one gates of mercy be opened is also found in *Maavor Yabok*. The verse "And He will cause him to dream, He will heal him, He will watch him, and He will revive him"[14] is also quoted in *Maavor Yabok* and becomes the biblical basis for the belief that dreams can awaken one to repentance.

The appeal, in this prayer from *Sefer HaHayiim*, for a perfect healing from the fourth palace (the fourth *Sefirah* of *Hesed*, Kindness) in which the Angel Raphael appears, is certainly a usage of kabbalistic imagery. Finally, there is an appeal to God's name אהיה אשר אהיה, (*Eheyeh Asher Eheyeh*) which has frequently been appealed to in *Maavor Yabok*.

I do not mean to infer that *Sefer HaHayiim* borrowed these verses and imagery from *Maavor Yabok*. I do want to suggest, however, that although the basic emphases of the works diverge, they were borrowing many prayers from a common circulating oral tradition, from both the kabbalistic as well as the more traditional rabbinic traditions. The latter seems to have been used more by

12. Ascher, *The Book of Life*, 143.
13. Ascher, *The Book of Life*, 145.
14. Ascher, *The Book of Life*, 145.

Sefer HaHayiim, whereas the former uses the kabbalistic sources extensively.

The final part in this section of prayers for the extremely ill, from *Sefer HaHayiim*, are prayers said for the sage, that is, the "student of wisdom," the Torah scholar. Two things should be mentioned here. The first is that the worthiness of Torah study and deeds of kindness are used for this appeal for long years and good health. The second is that the very straightforward biblical-rabbinic language of these prayers stands in marked contrast to the previously mentioned prayers said for and by the Torah scholar in *Maavor Yabok*. The florid mystical imagery of the latter is missing here in *Sefer HaHayiim*. There is only a direct appeal here to forgiveness of sins, and therefore God's healing through His mercy. There was most definitely a hierarchy within the Jewish community at this time as there were in both books special prayers offered for the sage.

Maavor Yabok

In the section in *Maavor Yabok* that follows the confessional section described earlier, a variety of prayers and customs are mentioned. In a sense, it is a miscellaneous section, which includes prayers for the extremely ill and those approaching *goses*, that is, the end of life.

There is a prayer, short in length, that one says if he or she feels that death is near, *haShahah dechokah* השעה דחוקה. The person who is extremely ill should spread his or her ten fingers toward heaven. The dying should then concentrate on a unity with the Holy One Praised be He and God's Presence, and say:

> In the light of the cause of causes, the first cause, who revives all by the foundation of the rising of his soul, he will say: 'Master of the universe, may it be Your will that my rest will be peaceful.' He will concentrate on the name of the Holy One, and God's unity, in the presence of the great and awesome Mt. Sinai.[15]

15. Berechiah, *Maavor*, 96.

Note the description of ritual and the reference to philosophical terms such as "first cause," the emphasis on the concentration on God's name, God's unity, and the revelation at Mount Sinai and the ensuing covenant. None of these elements are mentioned or included in *Sefer HaHayiim*. It also is interesting that this noticeably short prayer asks only for peacefulness, not for healing or for the rewards in the world to come. Although these other concepts might be implied, they are not explicitly stated. At the time of death, with all one's concomitant fears, it is only peace that is requested and desired. Quite often for the dying, it is this goal that is more desired than anything else as it would mean an end to whatever suffering he or she is experiencing.

The next prayer in this section of *Maavor Yabok* is said before the soul leaves the body. It is obviously out of chronological order because the prayers for the one nearing death (the one in a state of *goses*) do not enter the liturgy until later. The prayer is from the book of Isaiah 6:3:

> In the death of King Uzziah, I saw the Lord sitting on His high and exalted throne, and its limits filled the palace. Seraphim were standing over it, six wings for each one, by two its face was covered, by two its feet were covered, and by two it flew. And they called one to another, 'Holy, Holy, Holy is the Lord of Hosts, the whole earth is filled with His glory.'[16]

The commentary to this prayer explains that at death, the soul of the righteous returns to the highest World of Emanations אצילות (*Aztilut*), because the soul of the righteous is made from the intercourse of the *Sefirot Tiferet* and *Malchut*.[17] Because this prayer has forty-two letters from the word את (*et*) through the word כבודו (*k'vodo*), it is hoped that he who concentrates on these letters will receive worthiness from heaven "by the name א"ת which collects all the emanations from the Keter on high which is א (*aleph*) until Malchut which is ת (*tav*) that is אדוני."[18]

16. Berechiah, *Maavor*, 96.
17. Berechiah, *Maavor*, 181, 186.
18. Berechiah, *Maavor*, 187.

This comment is followed by a long commentary on each of the phrases of the previous verses from Isaiah. It presents how they bring together the ten *Sefirot*. It is specified that these forty-two letters must be concentrated on, and that each vowel must also be stressed.

It is then pointed out that he who concentrates:

> on the first kadosh (Holy) concentrates on the first three spheres Keter, Hochmah, and Binah; the second kadosh concentrates on the second three spheres Hesed, Gevurah, and Tipheret; and the third kadosh concentrates on the last three *Sefirot* Nezach, Hod, and Yesod. And 'The whole earth is filled with His glory' concentrates on the tenth sphere.[19]

Berechiah concludes his commentary on this prayer by discussing its theurgic function and its result in reference to what happens to one's soul and death:

> And surely all this will be a preparation to purify him and sanctify him, that he will be worthy to be a sweet-smelling offering to the Adonai and a pure meal offering on the day of his departure to the courts of the Adonai. The Seraphim, of six wings, by their wings will cover him and will lift him up on high. May it be God's will that he be worthy, be revived, and see length of days, and with all Israel he will praise God forever in this world and in the world to come, Amen. May it be God's will.[20]

This section of prayers in *Maavor Yabok* then tells where in this book customs and laws pertaining to the period of *goses* are found. It then suggests that during the visit to the sick person, the visitor should say:

> The Holy One Praised be He, may God take pity to receive you and bring you up by fullness of mercy. Master of the Universe do so because of Your kindness and because of Your great name. Do not put the sick one to

19. Berechiah, *Maavor*, 188.
20. Berechiah, *Maavor*, 188.

shame because of his thoughts and may all the sick of Israel be included in mercy.[21]

Sefer HaHayiim, in an earlier section, suggests that the following prayer be said upon leaving a sick person. This prayer is being discussed now because it is appropriate to see it compared with its counterpart in *Maavor Yabok* at this point in the text. The prayer in *Sefer HaHayiim* reads:

> On leaving the patient, say – 'O may God send thee a speedy and a perfect cure, and unto all the sick of Israel' On Sabbath or Festival the following should be said – 'This day of Sabbath (or festival) is a day of rest from grief and heart-rending prayer, yet recovery will speedily be granted unto thee, and unto all the sick of Israel, and thus celebrate the Sabbath in peace.'[22]

When these prayers are compared with those from *Maavor Yabok*, neither the Holy One Praised be He, God's Divine Presence, nor God's mercy is referred to in these prayers from *Sefer HaHayiim*, which became the accepted practice, whereas they appear in *Maavor Yabok*'s prayer.

Before another section of psalms in *Maavor Yabok*, it states that the sick person must see the sufferings that has come upon him or her as an atonement for the sins of his or her soul. It is important for this person to accept the sufferings in love before he or she is on the deathbed, knowing that they are sent out of God's mercy and love, to bring that person back into harmony with the *Sefirot*, and therefore God. Once again, this strategy against death, which is acceptance, is presented.

Berechiah then numerically lists twenty-eight psalms and suggests that one who is on his deathbed should recite these psalms, because they unify the twenty-eight camps of the Divine Presence. It states that the person can, however, recite as many or as few of these psalms as wanted. Although Berechiah does not say this, it is evident that the psalms to be recited, and the number

21. Berechiah, *Maavor*, 97.

22. Ascher, *The Book of Life*, 105.

said, were dictated by local customs, because the number to be read is not fixed. This is particularly interesting as he does state the number's more mystical significance.

Looking at three of the psalms in particular, Psalms 84, 120, and 123, they can be summarized by the following comments. Psalm 84 tells of yearnings by the Hasid for the courts of God where he will find safety and protection. Psalm 120 is a plea for salvation from one's enemies. Psalm 123 is a petition for the God's mercy. These three psalms, at least, continue in the tradition of the psalms quoted above, in that they express yearning for a relationship with God and Divine mercy.

As part of this miscellaneous section, Berechiah includes 112 verses from *Tanach* that are to be said by the sick one, or for him or her by visitors. The intention of these verses is to pass the fjord of Yabok, *Maavor Yabok* מעבר יבק from below to above, from this world to the world to come. Here, the image of the fjord, as with many other mythologies (i.e., River Styx in Greek mythology), represents the passage from life through death to the next world. Berechiah accomplished this through the number 112, (*kof, Yod, Bet*) קיב in Hebrew, which is, of course, a reversal of the letters יבק, Yabok, the name of the book.

Also, it is pointed out in the text that the three names of God, הוי"ה , אהי"ה אדנו"ת (*Havayah, Eheyeh, Adnut*), are numerically equivalent to the number 112, and therefore these verses have a theurgic influence on these names of God. Finally, this explanation of the metaphysical process behind the saying of 112 verses states that the spark from the soul of the person saying these verses attaches its strength to the other souls of the people of Israel, and therein it derives its strength.

The introduction to these verses sets this section's tone, which is one of hope in God's protection and presence:

> Harken heavens and I will speak, listen earth to the words of my mouth. My doctrine shall drop as the rain, my speech shall distill as the dew, as the small rain upon the tender grass, and as the showers upon the herb. The Lord of Hosts is with us, our rock, the God of Jacob, selah.

Lord of Hosts, happy is the man who trusts in You. Adonai, save, the Sovereign will answer on the day we call. You are my hiding-place. You will preserve me from the adversary with songs of deliverance. You will compass me about. Selah. Trust in Adonai always, because Jah, Adonai, is the eternal rock. Adonai will give strength to God's people, Adonai will bless God's people with peace. At God's right is Michael, God's left Gabriel, before God Raphael, behind God Nuriel, and above God's head the Divine spirt of God.[23]

All these 112 verses quoted from the *Tanach* continue the theme of this introduction. These 112 verses are divided into four sections. The first, which is not included in the total count because it is only an introduction and is not a name of God, is composed of twenty-one verses equivalent to the word אך (only). The second section is composed of twenty-six verses equivalent to God's name (*Eheyeh*) אהי"ה. The third section is composed of twenty-six verses equivalent to God's name (*Havayah*) הוי"ה, and the concluding section contains sixty-five verses, which is equivalent to third name of God, (*Adnut*) אדנו"ת. It is interesting that two sections of verses from the *Tanach* include descriptions of the priestly functions of atonement. Because these verses have a theurgic function, it could be said that just by reading such verses, the sick person receives benefits from their recitation, as if he or she were a priest performing such functions of atonement. As seen earlier, this is an example of the propitiatory strategy of prayer and the recitation of verses from *Tanach*.

The twenty-six verses in the second section, which are equivalent numerically to God's name הוי"ה (*Havayah*), contain verses from Isaiah that were quoted previously, but later were made a part of the *kedushah*, sanctification, prayer recited at worship services. This prayer, *Ana Bekoach*, is also found in the Kabbalat Shabbat service; its translation in the siddur edited by David De Sola Pool is:

We pray Thee, God, free captive Israel
Through Thy right hand's mighty power.

23. Berechiah, *Maavor*, 98.

God of awe, receive Thy people's prayer;
Uplift us, make us pure.
Almighty God, we pray Thee,
Guard as the apple of the eye those who seek Thy unity.
Bless us, cleanse us,
And ever temper for us Thy justice with Thy mercy.
Almighty and Holy,
Lead on Thy flock in Thy bountiful goodness.
Supreme and only God,
Turn to Thy people who are mindful of Thy holiness.
Accept our prayer, give ear to our cry,
Thou who knowest our inward thoughts.
Blessed be His glorious and sovereign name forever
and ever.[24]

This prayer אנא בכח (*Ana Bakoach*) is also found in Isaiah Horowitz's work, *Shnei Luehot Habrit* which was printed in 1649. Concerning the importance and function of this prayer as the sick person nears the stage of *goses*, Horowitz writes:

> This ancient prayer is based on the Name of forty-two letters, and Rabbi Simon ben Yohai, may his memory be for a blessing, wrote in the work HaPardes in the gate 'specifics of the names' at the end of parasha 13, that every name has six letters equivalent to the six wings of Seraphim, and based on this it is said 'six wings, six wings, two for each' (in Isaiah). And he said that is good to mention this name before one goes to sleep, and thus too for one close to his demise, that upon these six wings it is written in Isaiah, 'with two he will cover his feet, and with two he will fly' the soul above, and will be worthy to be saved from the Destructive Angels and from all demons and will be worthy of the life of the world to come, this ends the quotation. And I received from the watchers of the dead who sit around him, from the moment of death until he will be covered with earth in the grave, they will sit in successive watches around him, diligently, that profane air will not enter among them. And they mention this prayer continually without

24. de Sola Pool, *The Traditional Prayer Book for Sabbath and Festivals*, 40.

a moment's stop, and they will not say it less than one thousand times.[25]

Dr. Jacob Marcus states that this prayer was attributed to the first-century Tanna Nehunya ben Ha-Kannah, [26] Of the prayer, he writes:

> One of the most frequently recurring prayer formulas in the extended ritual for the sick is the ana ba-koah prayer. ... As one recited this brief forty-two-word cabbalistic prayer – or its variations – one was asked to think of the initial letters of each word. All told there are forty-two initial letters, which is also the total number of letters in God's four merciful Names when spelt out fully: Aleph, dalet, nun, yod; he waw yod he; aleph he yod he; yod he waw he. It is this forty-two letter Name of God that has the power to save the soul from the evil spirits. Each line of this seven-line prayer of Nehunya has six initial letters for its six words. These letters form a word on which one must mentally concentrate. The initial letters of the second line, for instance, serve as an invocation against Satan when the soul leaves the body. Each mystical word, formed from the initial letters of each one of the six words on each line, corresponds to the six wings of the divine creatures described in Isaiah 6. By means of these wings the soul flies upward to God and merits being saved from the angels of destruction and becoming worthy of the life of the world to come.[27]

25. Horowitz, *Shenei Luehot Habrit*, Part II, 4c.
26. Marcus, *Communal Sick-Care*, 267.
27. Marcus, *Communal Sick-Care*, 268.

82

Chapter VII

<><><><><><><><><><><><><><><><><><><><><><><><><><><><><><><><><><><><><>

AS DEATH APPROACHES

Maavor Yabok

AS THE TIME OF the departure of the soul from the body approaches, a prayer in *Maavor Yabok* is said by those standing over a "great man" (great Torah scholar).[1] If it is at night, the "thirteen attributes" of God may be added. The prayer is composed of twenty-six verses that, as written above, are equivalent numerically to God's name (*Havayah*) הוי״ה, which adds another theurgic device to the liturgy. *Maavor Yabok* contains more prayers written specifically for the "student of wisdom" and the "great man" than does *Sefer HaHayiim*. This prayer is composed of verses from the *Tanach*. The first verse is a play on the words "Jacob went his way," from Genesis 32:2. This biblical section speaks of Jacob's taking leave of Laban, and it tells how God's angels met him and protected him. The verse sets this theme of God's protection of the sick person who is dying, which carries over into the next quoted verse, Exodus 23:20. This prayer then quotes the sacrificial service for the consecration of the priests, which comes from the Torah.

By reading these verses, a sick person vicariously puts himself or herself into the position of the High Priest Aaron, who serves before God. This is followed by verses that tell of the improper

---

1. Berechiah, *Maavor*, 104.

service of Aaron's sons and their deaths. The verse "And Moses said, 'Arise Adonai and scatter Your enemies, and Your enemies shall flee before You'"[2] follows. These verses imply that improper service before God will bring on punishment and death. This warning becomes an incentive to do proper atonement, which is performed by reading these propitiatory and confessional prayers. If this a warning for the person who is praying these prayers, it can be quite overwhelming in terms of its implications related to the correct offering of these prayers and rituals.

This prayer concludes with verses from the Writings from *Tanach* in which God established Divine protection for Israel, and therefore with the sick one. The *kedushah* verses from Isaiah are once again quoted. This petition for God's protection becomes one of the major themes of the concluding section of prayers, which begins with the prayer תפלה לעני, "prayer for the lowly one." Such words at this time in the dying process can be seen as being of great comfort to the one offering them.

This prayer begins with an appeal to God, whose name is (*Eheyeh Asher Eheyeh*) אהיה אשר אהיה. This name of God is synonymous with God's mercy, because this prayer and the previous prayers that mention this name, invariably appeal to God's quality of forgiveness. God is the "God of all spirits" אלוהי הרוחות and gives a pure soul to God's people, revives the living, brings up the fallen, revives the sick, and causes death by mercy. It is interesting how this prayer addresses itself to the attributes of God that would be pertinent to the one in *goses*, the one for whom the prayer is said. The term "causes death by mercy"[3] is also interesting. It is not biblical. Such an outlook would help one to accept death, because it is seen as a merciful action on God's part. Such knowledge could have as much value and comfort, if not more so, than the knowledge that God "causes death by justice."

The prayer then appeals directly to God's mercy by mentioning the sick one's name. In very realistic terms, it describes his or her condition to God, as a person

2. Berechiah, *Maavor, 104.*

3. Berechiah, *Maavor, 105.*

who wails from his groaning heart and not from the pu-
rity of his flesh. His heart flutters and his strength fails
him.[4]

The prayer hopes that this one's soul is precious in God's sight,
and that it will be released from its prison so that it can praise God.
Such praise can be said only if death is overcome and/or an im-
mortal life with God is achieved.

As seen with these prayers, first healing is prayed for: that is,
before the imminence of death is accepted. As in the prayer from
Sefer HaHayiim, see Chapter VI, an appeal is made to the angel
Raphael in the fourth palace. Unlike the prayer in *Sefer HaHayiim*,
however, *Maavor Yabok* embellishes this prayer with more kab-
balistic imagery:

> And from the light which lights from the east, from the
> fourth palace, his name is Raphael. It is he, whom You
> have commanded, by the strength of Your name אהי"ה ,
> for the good of Israel, and to shine upon them to revive
> the sick from their sickness and to save from their evil.[5]

As was also seen above, if death must come, it is hoped that
the soul will be saved. It is petitioned that a spirit of purity and
holiness will be added to the sick one's soul, and that he or she will
be able to receive God's chastisements in love.

Then, the "good death" is described. The prayer hopes that the
dying one will be worthy of seeing the residence of God's dwelling.
It is implied from these materials and from what follows that this
state and relationship with God comes from a purity of soul, which
has been achieved before death through earnest repentance. It is
also hoped that one's nefesh, ruach, and neshamah will join in the
light of the Divine Presence, and with the four angels appointed
from the sixth palace (*Tiferet*).

The soul should leave by a kiss, and it should be protected
from all evil spirits, especially those that rule the Dark Side סטרא
(Sitra Achra) אחרא. It is hoped that God will prepare an altar from

4. Berechiah, *Maavor,* 105.
5. Berechiah, *Maavor,* 105.

the cedars of Lebanon for the offering of this soul, and that it will enter the gates of mercy and the Garden of Eden. A beautiful description of the eternal life is found in the words:

> And he will sing God's glory unto You in the Garden of Eden, not to be silent, with the souls of Your righteous who sit before You, the crown of their light upon their head, to be given benefit from the light of Your face. And may length of days, years and peace be added unto us with great strength and might with all Israel, comrades, amen. Thus, may it be Your will.[6]

Whereas *Sefer HaHayiim* also describes this idea that if death must come, it should be a "good death" ("the kiss of death") in which the soul enters the Garden of Eden, nowhere does *Sefer HaHayiim* contain such an involved description of the "good death" as is described here in *Maavor Yabok*. That such a prayer is said before one is in the state of *goses* speaks of its assumed physical and spiritual efficacy. By these prayers, the visitor is able to do something even in the face of the death for the dying person being visited. This helps to overcome the feeling of helplessness often experienced by friends, families, and community members:

> And he will stress by the word כן the unity of Wisdom and Understanding. רצוֹץ of the exalted Crown pours upon them from the goodness by hidden knowledge *Ayn Sof*[7]

What an incredible appreciation of the power and effect of words! *Sefer HaHayiim* does not relate to these texts in the same theosophical and kabbalistic language as does *Maavor Yabok*.

The text of *Maavor Yabok* then attributes to Moses this statement before his death: "Blessed is God's name who lives and exists forever."[8] The text gives the directive: "And from this every man

---

6. Berechiah, *Maavor,* 106.

7. Berechiah, *Maavor,* 106.

8. Berechiah, *Maavor,* 106.

will learn."[9] It is interesting that such a statement is not made by Moses in the biblical text but is found in the psalms.

Also, Berechiah's note directs this acceptance of the eternality of God to every person by stating that everyone should learn from this statement. This directive has great force because it is read for the one in *goses*. The statement implies that a person must recognize his finiteness and God's infiniteness, and thus placing himself or herself, at the time of death, into God's hands. This hope in God's protective power is emphasized in the remaining prayers before death.

The next prayer, הגואל המלך (*Ha-Melech Ha-Goel*), is composed of biblical verses. It begins with the well-known prayer of Jacob:

> The angel who redeems me, from all evil, may he bless the boys, and may they be called by called by my name and the name of my fathers, Abraham and Jacob, and may they increase greatly over the earth.[10]

The rubric to this prayer suggests that, if possible, this prayer should be read by the one in *goses*. These verses suggest the biblical idea of the eternality of one's name through one's progeny. In this sense, one achieves what can be called social immortality. This hope in social immortality, however, is extended to a hope in actual personal immortality, because one places himself or herself into God's hands:

> Save my soul from the sword, and my uniqueness from the dog . . . into the hand of Adonai may I fall, for God's mercies are great, but not into the hand of man. Into Your hand will I commend my spirit, You will redeem me O Adonai, God of Truth. In goodness you will sleep, and you will awake in good mercy, amen. . . . I will walk before the Adonai in the Lands of the Living. . . . And in righteousness will behold Your face, and I will be satisfied in the awakening of Your visage. Every soul will praise, Jah, they will praise Jah. God of our salvation help

9. Berechiah, *Maavor, 104.*

10. Berechiah, *Maavor, 107.*

us by the glory of Your name. God is merciful, forgiving
iniquity, and God will not destroy. Frequently God turns
God's anger away and does not stir up all God's wrath.
Hear O Israel, Adonai our God, Adonai is One. Blessed
be God's name whose glorious kingdom is forever and
forever . . .[11]

This prayer emphasizes God's mercy and God's protective
power. The prayer directs itself toward immortality. This is espe-
cially evident in the verse "In goodness you will sleep, and you will
awake in God's mercy, amen."[12] The phrase "in the Lands of the
Living" could refer to the social immortality of people, implied in
the opening quotation. The concluding verses imply a life, after the
event of death, with God:

Adonai is Sovereign, Adonai reigns, Adonai will reign
forever. Adonai, Adonai, is God, Adonai, Adonai, is God.
Specifically, אהי״ה אשר אהי״ה . God was, God is, and
God will be. God causes death and causes life. No god
was created before God and there will be none after God.
Do this for Your name. Do this for Your Torah. Do this
for Your holiness. That now I lie down, and I will awaken,
I sleep but then there will be peace for me.[13]

The next prayer, לך כי שליחך (lech ke sh'lechacha), is said by
those standing around the dying person. This prayer also begins
with verses calling for God's mercies. It includes the Priestly Bene-
diction from the biblical book of Numbers, and the prayer from the
"Service Saying the Shema Before Going to Sleep," in which God's
angels and protective spirit are called upon. The verse "Be strong
and of good courage, do not be frightened or afraid for Adonai is
with you wherever you go"[14] would be psychologically comforting
for the dying person, because he or she now is assured that one is
not alone, even at this time of death. It is important, however, for
this prayer to be said even if the one in goses seems not to be able

11. Berechiah, *Maavor,* 107.

12. Berechiah, *Maavor,* 107.

13. Berechiah, *Maavor,* 108.

14. Berechiah, *Maavor,* 108.

to hear the prayers. It is well-known that the last of the senses to go is the sense of hearing. The prayer then influences the soul of the dying as well as those whose who are reading it.

The verse:

> Why are You cast down my soul? And what meanest within me? Hope You in God; for I shall yet praise God, the salvation of my countenance and my God.[15]

also expresses the hope, by the sick person, for God's protection.

Then, the section from the Torah that describes the service of priestly offerings for atonement is mentioned. As seen earlier, one reads the verses concerning offerings to propitiate God vicariously.

The remainder of this prayer is composed of verses that continue to express the desire for God's mercy and protection. Included in this section are the biblical verses of the "thirteen attributes" and the section from Isaiah describing the wings of the seraphim, which appeared in the previous prayers.

Following is this prayer, which reads like a *piyyut* or poem:

> And God will ride upon a cherub, and God will fly, fly upon the wings of the wind. Kiss me from the kisses of God's mouth that Your love making is better than wine. O God, Adonai speak and call the earth from the east of the sun until its going down. Your perfection of the beauty of God appeared from Zion. Hear O Israel, Adonai Our God, Adonai is One. Adonai, God is God. Adonai is Sovereign. Adonai reigned. Adonai will reign forever.[16]

The first paragraph of this prayer expresses the desire of the dying person for the Garden of Eden, in which one's relationship with God is brought closer. Note should be taken of the phrase "I will be in Eden," which becomes a desired state. In this piyyut, as in the previously discussed prayer אנא בכח (*Ana B'Koach*), there are six words per line, which are broken into two words per grouping. The first letter of each group of three words spells out the abbreviation of a demonic spirit. Because I have been unable to find

---

15. Berechiah, *Maavor*, 108.
16. Berechiah, *Maavor*, 109.

mention of this poem in any other source and Berechiah does not cite a source, I would assume that he wrote it. Its sheer poetry and imagery would be most comforting to someone who is dying.

The second paragraph of verses from Song of Songs emphasizes one's relationship with God and upon the "kiss of death." Modern readers might call this an "easy death," a going-out of the soul. This can be seen as the hope that God will take one's soul into the Garden of Eden and there find enteral peace.

The use of sexual imagery, by the quotations from Song of Songs, at the time of death is also quite intriguing. Here, during the solemnity and emotions of the dying experience, love is expressed: that is, love between the dying person and God. This love between the two partners, which if the analogy may be extended, is consummated in death, concludes with the verses from the *Shema*.

The section of prayer from here until the moment of death is appropriately called the "verses of unity, consummation." This extends the imagery of *Yichud*, which is one of the most basic of kabbalistic methods to achieve, a unity with the Divine. The word *Yichud* itself refers to the *Yichud*, the sexual union of the husband and wife on their marital night. As one performs a *Yichud* through meditation on the names of God associated with the various *Sefirot*, the kabbalistic practitioner can bring about a unification of these *Sefirot* to achieve the desired end expressed through the words of prayer or the ritual itself, which is the desired achievement culminating in the peaceful death.

The last words of this prayer sound very much like the concluding verses of the *Neilah* service on Yom Kippur that mark the end of this holy day. The usage of these verses and their connection to this service would also give comfort to the dying person. The kabbalistic dynamics of these important verses are described in the following quotation from *Maavor Yabok*. Again, the effect of the verses upon the harmony of the *Sefirot* is emphasized, which influences the godhead:

> The creator made the harmony in the higher worlds dependent upon the lower worlds, and therefore the higher worlds are not separated from the lower as it is written

'And he will ride upon the cherub, and he will fly.' First
the spheres ride on Malchut to harmonize it, and after,
'and he will fly upon wings of the wind', and with the
verse 'and He will kiss me from the kisses of His mouth
that His love making is from the kisses of His mouth that
His love making is better than wine', and thus 'and Jacob
kissed Rachel and he raised his voice and cried'; here
there are seven worlds hinting at the seven kisses, seven
breaths, that masculine clings to feminine, feminine to
masculine, spirit with spirit, love with Foundation, and
they are the foundation of seven and the seven which
are spread out. 'And he will ride upon the cherubs, and
he will fly' 'kiss me from the kisses of His mouth' 'God,
O God, Adonai' "from Zion perfection of beauty' 'Hear
O Israel' 'Adonai, God, is God, Adonai is One and Ado-
nai's name is One.' The Unity needs to join two hundred
and forty-eight holy groups that they are by themselves
from themselves to themselves and therefore 'Adonai is
One' is connected with the Foundation letters יהו"ה . . .
the Foundation of Unity of 'Hear O Israel' which is the
connection of Ayn Sof with the spheres and afterward is
joined with them by Yesod.[17]

Aside from the description of theosophical and theurgical
activity of each word of this prayer, the opening sentence shows
the kabbalistic system's stress on the ability of a person to connect
with the upper divine system of *Sefirot* directly.

After this *piyyut* and these "verses of unification," various
psalms are recited. The *Shema*, which contains the customary and
important words to be said at the time of death, does not stand
by itself, as it does in *Sefer HaHayiim*. Instead, it is part of other
biblical verses ("verses of unification") and psalms. This arrange-
ment does not necessarily detract from the *Shema*; if anything, it
expands its basic idea of the unity with God.

Psalm 3 is written out in the text of *Maavor Yabok*.[18] Quite
a few aspects of this psalm would be appropriate for the last mo-
ments of one's life. In the first stanza:

17. Berechiah, *Maavor*, 418–419.
18. Berechiah, *Maavor*, 109–110.

Adonai, how many are mine adversaries become!
Many are they that rise up against me.
Many there are that say of my soul:
'There is no salvation for him in God.' Selah.[19]

The "adversaries" can be seen as sickness and death, because sickness and death seem to say, "there is no God." Yet, the dying person knows "You, O Adonai, are a shield about me. . . . I lay me down, and I sleep; I awake, for Adonai sustains me. . . . Arise O Adonai; save me, O my God."[20] The phrase "I awake for Adonai sustains me" might point to the concept of and hope in immortality, which, in the context of *Maavor Yabok*, is a continued existence in the Garden of Eden.

The text then suggests that Psalm 116 be read. This Psalm is also a supplication for God's salvation in the face of death:

I love that Adonai should hear
My voice and my supplications . . .
The cords of death compassed me,
And the straits of the nether-world
get hold upon me.
I found trouble and sorrow
But I called upon the name of Adonai.[21]

As seen in the words of this Psalm, the realities of death are never evaded, but are confronted, internalized, and visualized.

It is then suggested that the previously mentioned prayer be read. The next statement implies that the prayers over the person in *goses* will move visitors to repentance, which in turn will be beneficial to the dying person:

One can add 'the dwellers in clay' to hasten those standing there to repentance, that by this there will be worthiness for the departing one if they will be awakened to return from their way.[22]

19. Berechiah, *Maavor, 109–110.*
20. Berechiah, *Maavor, 109–110.*
21. Berechiah, *Maavor,* 110.
22. Berechiah, *Maavor,* 110.

This powerful spiritual effect of participation in the dying process with the dying person is remarkably interesting because it offers an incredible benefit to participate in this mitzvah.

The *piyyut*, "The Dwellers in Clay," by Solomon ibn Gabriol, is an exhortation for the Day of Atonement. It contains the strongest language of a person's sinful nature of any prayers analyzed thus far. As mentioned, its intended goal is to frighten a person into repentance, because it reveals this person's actual lowly nature:

> O habitants of homes of clay,
> Why lift ye such a swelling eye,
> What do ye boast of more than they? . . .
> To be unborn were better worth
> Then thus to reap distress and pain,
> For how easy great things to gain
> When struggling in this snare of earth?[23]

It implores the person to repent so that God can hide the Divine wrath and reveal God's mercy:

> O let the wicked turn aside,
> And take, O King, the path to Thee.
> Perchance the Rock will heed the plea.
> And from His wrath the sinner hide.[24]

The *piyyut*, as quoted in *Maavor Yabok*, then stops two stanzas short. These last two stanzas are placed in the next section, which is preceded by the statement that if the person is saying this only for himself, he or she should say the following, also from Gabriol's poem:

> Thou Ruler of the depth and height
> Stiff-necked were we in Thy despite,
> Yet of Thy mercies bate no wit
> But shed Thy sweet compassion o'er
> The people knocking at Thy gate,
> Thou art the Master of our fate,

23. Zangwill, trans., *Selected Religious Poems*, 61–62.
24. Zangwill, trans., *Selected Religious Poems*, 62.

And unto Thee our eyes upsoar.[25]

By this division of the *piyyut*, Berechiah shows a real sense of the text and its psychological function. Berechiah understands the human condition in which people know of their sinful nature. He uses the words of the poet to express the hope that despite this sinful nature there is hope in the knowledge that God is merciful and forgiving.

He then combines these verses of Gabriol's, appealing to God's mercies, with the beautiful verses of Abraham ibn Ezra, which follow through the previously established image of the Garden of Eden, appealing to God's forgiveness:

> Send out Angels of kindness
> and may they go out close by him,
> And peace to you who comes they will say
> with one voice to he who comes,
> And they will bring him to Thy Garden of Eden
> and there His throne will be.
> And he will be refined in Thy light
> and find the glory of his rest,
> And the light hidden before Thee
> will be his secret and his protection,
> And under the Shadow of Thy wings
> his protective screen will be given him,
> With the help of God who shows mercy and forgiveness
> to answer His people and congregation.[26]

Berechiah concludes this section of "verses at the time of the going out of the soul" with various comments on the moment of death. He states that one whose soul is ordained to depart should have the intention of a slaughterer of sacrifices, as explained in Maimonides' *Mishneh Torah*, Chapter 2, *Hilchot Maaseh HaCarbanot*.[27] The sick person and the dying person see their confession and death as an atonement (sacrifice) for sins.

25. Zangwill, trans., *Selected Religious Poems*, 63.
26. Berechiah, *Maavor*, 111.
27. Berechiah, *Maavor, 111.*

Berechiah then writes that it is good when one can die while hearing or saying verses of mercy and thoughts of Torah. These thoughts will bring help from heaven and secure one's departure, as described earlier. Berechiah also writes that the dying person should try to fulfill any commandments that he or she can and should seek forgiveness from anyone wronged. A person should accept death willingly. Berechiah suggests various petitions to be said at morning, afternoon, and evening. These include verses of "mercy"[28] from the *Tanach*.

This concludes the discussion of this section of *Maavor Yabok*. One's religious life remains active until the very last moment of life: that is, one's relationship between a person and God, and among persons. There is no concept of the modern idea of disengagement, at least from God, at the time of dying and death.

Sefer HaHayiim

Before the prayers for the person who is dying, *goses*, in *Sefer HaHayiim*, there are sections that contain blessings of thanksgiving for recovery from illness, the changing of one's name, and a paternal blessing before death. The "ritual for changing one's name." (*Sh'nui HaShem*) is unlike other prayers previously looked at in this book. It represents a strategy to avoid death by deceiving God and the Angel of Death. This is accomplished by changing one's name and therefore disguising a person's soul from whatever is in store for it.

The "paternal blessing before death" is composed of the blessing of Jacob over his grandsons, with the priestly benediction and the following verses added:

> Place upon him the spirit of the Lord, the spirit of wisdom and understanding, the spirit of advice and strength, the spirit of knowledge and fear of the Lord.[29]

28. Berechiah, *Maavor*, 111.
29. Ascher, *The Book of Life*, 163.

Such a ritual would be comforting to a dying person because he or she would feel the continuity of heritage by bestowing these blessings upon the person's children before the person's death. The dying one might visualize or feel the presence of his or her own parents offering their blessing at this time.

After these miscellaneous prayers, *Sefer HaHayiim* adds:

> Rabbi Simon, son of Yochai, says, As soon as those who attend the sick person perceive that he draws near to the end of all flesh, it becomes their imperative duty to make him aware of it, and to inform him that the hour is at hand when he will be called to appear before the throne of the Most High Judge, and that the time has arrived to reconcile himself with his Heavenly Father. Man may, in one moment, by one pious deed, acquire eternal life. . . . He must, therefore, as soon as we perceive that the illness of the sufferer increases, much more when cure becomes hopeless, call his attention to his serious condition . . . we terminate our earthly career in the spirit and words of Holy Write, 'Till I give up my ghost, I will not remove my integrity from me.'[30]

The idea of protecting one from the reality of his or her death, as practiced by some, is absent in this passage. A person's integrity is not lost when a strategy is presented to meet and overcome death by the person himself or herself standing strong before death.

Concerning this way to face death, the text later states:

> When the patient perceived that his time to die draws near, he should with a pious spirit and a humble heart accept the heavenly decree . . . and offer thanks to the name of God, for having granted him to die undisturbedly on his bed . . . and thus breathe his last in the firm belief in the Unity of the only God of Israel.[31]

These words have the dying person express true faith in God as he or she is preparing to take that last breath. This could be seen

---

30. Ascher, *The Book of Life*, 162–163.

31. Ascher, *The Book of Life*, 167.

as describing for this book a "good" death, about which both *Sefer HaHayiim* and *Maavor Yabok* agree.

As stated in *Sefer HaHayiim*,

> That the gates of heaven may be opened to receive his devotion, and that his soul may undisturbedly soar to the heavenly abode in the garden of Eden, there to enjoy, beneath the tree of eternal life, the plentitude of bliss treasured up for the righteous. Of such a death King Solomon says, 'That the day of death is better than the day of birth.' Indeed, such a departure from life may justly be termed good: as the sages (of blessed memory) comment on the verse: 'And God saw everything that He had made, and behold it was very good.' The words 'very good,' they say, allude to death; when the truly pious and virtuous receive their full reward in the higher regions, and enjoy the celestial and undisturbed tranquility of the soul, figuratively termed by our sages, the day which is completely Sabbath.[32]

The prayers said either by the person in *goses*, if possible, or by others for him or her, are found in the section "And this is the Gate of Heaven."[33] While the explanatory section preceding this prayer appears to be of a kabbalistic nature, because it is based on number play, no references are given and it is not in parentheses, as were the earlier kabbalistic statements found in *Sefer HaHayiim*.

> It is said that the eighteen worlds through which the soul descends at birth and the eighteen worlds through which the soul ascends at death are referred to in the eighteen verses of the first prayer פתחו לי (*Pitchu Li*). This occurs in order that the soul cleaves to the living God and is worthy of the resurrection to be, that 'you that cleave to the Lord your God, all of you are living this day,' that the righteous even in their death are called living.[34]

32. Ascher, *The Book of Life*, 168.
33. Ascher, *The Book of Life*, 169.
34. Ascher, *The Book of Life*, 169.

Note the interesting phrase "that the righteous even in their death are called living." Moreover, this is one of the few places in both *Sefer HaHayiim* and *Maavor Yabok* that the term "resurrection" is mentioned.

This prayer is a beautiful collection of verses that contain the word "gate" in them or express the relationship between God and the one for whom God opens the gates (the dying person):

> Open to me the gates of righteousness; I will enter there, and I will thank the Eternal. . . . I sleep, but my heart waketh; it is the voice of my beloved that knocketh, saying, open to me, my sister, my love, my dove, my undefiled; for my head is filled with dew, and my locks with the drops of the night . . . to hear the groaning of the prisoner, to lose those that are appointed to death. . . . Thou wilt show me the path of life; in Thy presence is fulness of joy, in Thy right hand there is beatitude for evermore.[35]

The Psalm for the Sabbath Day is then recited. In the preceding explanatory remarks, the verse "the righteous shall flourish like the palm-tree; he shall grow like the cedar in Lebanon"[36] refers to the growth and ascension of the soul up through the eighteen worlds to God. This also points to the concept of resurrection.

The next paragraph[37] contains the verse that in *Maavor Yabok* was included in the "verses of unification," "Let Him kiss me with the kisses of His mouth for thy love is better than wine"[38] This paragraph continues the hope for immortality in relationship with God. Before that, however, there is a recognition of the closeness and reality of death:

> For I know that Thou wilt bring me to death, and to the house appointed for all the living. Gather not my soul with sinners, nor my life with bloody men. Yea, though I walk through the valley of the shadow of death,—I will fear no evil. . . . As for me I will behold Thy face in

35. Ascher, *The Book of Life*, 169–170.
36. Ascher, *The Book of Life*, 171
37. Ascher, *The Book of Life*, 172.
38. Ascher, *The Book of Life*, 173.

righteousness; awaking I shall feast on Thy glory. For this God is our God for ever and ever; He will be our guide even beyond death. For Thy salvation I have waited O Eternal.[39]

The next prayer, אנא אדוני (Ana Adonai), continues this theme when it states:

the moment has now arrived at which I have to return to Thee the soul which Thou hast deposited within me. Take it back from me by the kiss of Thy mouth, and not by the angel of death . . . send Thy angels of mercy and truth to attend to the last moment of my existence, to receive my soul, and to restore her to her heavenly source – the garden of Eden.[40]

Note the difference between the kiss of death and the visitation of the Angel of Death. One represents an "easy" death, whereas the other is a "difficult" death.

The second part of this prayer is a confession, in which because there is a confession of sins, God will not doom his

soul to perdition but grant me a portion in the garden of Eden, in the assembly of the saints and pious ones. Deign that I may be worthy of participating in the resurrection of the dead, and in the tranquil bliss of a future world, which is a one and everlasting Sabbath.[41]

Again, *Sefer HaHayiim* mentions resurrection. Rabbinic eschatology, as demonstrated so often in *Sefer HaHayiim*, sees the Day of Judgment as significant, and therefore also resurrection, whereas the kabbalistic system, as demonstrated in *Maavor Yabok*, sees a harmony of the soul with the *Sefirot* as the desired goal after death. It is also possible that *Maavor Yabok*, as a kabbalistic text, puts more emphasis on *gilgul*, which is reincarnation, and the need for the soul to continue an eternal path leading to the repair of the sins that complete the soul's journey.

39. Ascher, *The Book of Life*, 173.
40. Ascher, *The Book of Life*, 173–175.
41. Ascher, *The Book of Life*, 175.

A reading of the two works reveals that they both discuss the transmigration of the soul. *Sefer HaHayiim* does this in its kabbalistic and non-rabbinic sections. Both books also discuss the image of the Garden of Eden. They infrequently and sparsely mention and discuss *Gehinom*, which is the lower world from the Garden of Eden. Only *Sefer HaHayiim* mentions the term "resurrection" at all. One reason for the infrequent mention of "resurrection" might be that these books assume that the term "Garden of Eden" subsumes "resurrection."

Another possibility is that terms such as "*Gehinom*," "transmigration," and "resurrection" conjure an image of stern judgment and therefore "fear and trembling" in the reader. Both works have a person who is ill and a person who is dying reflecting upon sin and their sinful nature to inspire repentance before death. These books then attempt to offer the reward that waits for the repentant. The reason for the frequent image of the Garden of Eden over other ones such as *Gehinom* is that the Garden image is really the only positive one.

Sefer HaHayiim includes quotations of Rabbi Jochanan and Rabbi Simeon, son of Yochai, which stress the importance of a good life and a good reputation, even until the very moment of death:

> But happy that man . . . who, to the last hour of his existence, maintained the good reputation acquired from early youth. To him may be applied the maxim of the wisest of kings: "A good name is better than a precious ointment, and the day of death than the day of one's birth."[42]

The next prayer, אל אדוני (*El Adonai*), whose importance was emphasized earlier, is like the prayer in *Maavor Yabok* תפלה לעני (*Tefillah L'Ani*), also discussed previously. There is first an appeal to God's mercy for healing from sickness. The prayer is that if death must come, it should be a death of peace, accompanied by an entrance into the Garden of Eden.

---

42. Ascher, *The Book of Life*, 175.

The same themes as those in the section concerning the prayers of the person in *goses* continue in the following pages.

The first prayer, אלהים יסעדך (*Elohim Yisadehchah*), is a piyyut. Each line contains five words equivalent in number to the five levels of the soul, נפש רוח נשמה חיה יחידה (*Nefesh, Ruach, Neshamah, Chayah, Y'chidah*) and the five books of the Torah. The alphabet is cited twice, with each letter beginning a line. First, the alphabet is cited in its normal order, and then in reverse. This repetition of the alphabet is performed so that it represents both the written and the oral Torah; this is explained in the explanatory note that precedes the text.

This *piyyut* praises the rewards of the righteous person in the world to come. It gives solace to the dying person by informing him of what lies ahead:

> Exclaim aloud, Eternal God, who is like unto Thee? and surely, he will reward thee with abundance of delight and celestial bliss.
>
> Great and heavenly reward awaits thee; in full age thou shalt come to the repose of thine ancestors.
>
> The law which thou didst practice, the faith in which thou didst live, will be thy guardians; watched by them thou wilt sweetly and undisturbedly sleep.
>
> The Omnipotent God has formed thee, and appointed thy lot: surely the day of thy death is better than that of thy birth.
>
> In that higher region of blissfulness thou wilt continue to live an everlasting life; this will be the reward for thine earthly labour.
>
> How thine immortal soul will live – live for eternity; such will be thy life, and the length of thy days.[43]

The next prayer, יהי כבוד (*Y'hi Kavod*), uses verses from the *Tanach* to declare God's righteousness, mercy, and power over life. This knowledge gives the dying person hope. God's consistent righteousness and faithfulness give the dying person the knowledge that he or she will not be forsaken:

---

43. Ascher, *The Book of Life*, 179–181.

I will sing of mercy and judgement; unto Thee, O Eternal, will I sing. For the righteous God loveth righteousness; His countenance doth graciously behold the upright. But Thou art the same, and Thy years shall have no end. Why art Thou cast down, O my soul? and why art Thou disquieted in me? Hope, Thou in God: for I shall yet praise Him for the salvation of His countenance. After two days (of affliction) will He revive us: on the third day He will establish, that we shall live in His presence.[44]

The final prayer, צדקתך (*Tzidketchah*), expresses hope for life eternal, based first on God's righteousness, and then on God's mercy:

The righteousness is an everlasting righteousness, and Thy law the everlasting truth. For this is God our God, for ever and ever: He will be our guide even beyond death. As for God, His way is immutable, the word of the Eternal is tried: He is a buckler to all those who trust in Him. . . . the days of our years are seventy; and if in strength they be eighty years, yet is their pride labour and sorrow; for it is soon cut off and we fly away. But they that wait upon the Eternal shall renew their strength . . . who redeemeth thy life from destruction; who crowneth thee with loving-kindness and tender mercies. . . . All flesh shall perish together, and man shall return unto dust. . . . The Eternal killeth and maketh alive: He bringeth down to the grave and bringeth up. Wilt Thou, not return and revive us? that Thy people may rejoice in Thee. Let Israel, therefore, trust in the Eternal: for the Eternal there is mercy, and with Him is plenteous redemption.[45]

Even in these final prayers, the difference between the two works under discussion can be seen. Whereas *Sefer HaHayiim* speaks of God's mercy, it emphasizes God's judgment, which is lacking in the closing section of *Maavor Yabok*. In *Sefer HaHayiim*, the life in the world to come and resurrection are viewed as rewards. *Maavor Yabok* explicitly and implicitly speaks of the world

44. Ascher, *The Book of Life*, 187.
45. Ascher, *The Book of Life*, 187–191.

to come, not in terms of rewards, which might be why it speaks only of the Garden of Eden and not resurrection, but in terms of harmony with God, to be bathed in God's light through the redressed balance in the *Sefirot*.

Each work, during their last sections, views the "kiss of God" as the "good" death. Each work, however, has its own language and imagery for describing that kiss. The difference, I contend, lies in the difference between the understanding and vocabulary the rabbinic and the kabbalistic systems had of God and God's relationship to each person.

Sefer HaHayiim concludes with well-known prayers and hymns, יגדל (*Yigdal*) and אדון עולם (*Adon Olam*), and the verses of "unification." *Maavor Yabok* has none of these hymns. As to these verses of "unification," they are presented alone and not with surrounding verses, as is the case in *Maavor Yabok*. Again, the kabbalistic references and underpinning are not present in most of *Sefer HaHayiim*.

Chapter VIII

⁓⁓

REFLECTIONS

THIS JOURNEY THROUGH THE 17th-century text *Maavor Yabok* and the 18th-century text *Sefer HaHayiim* and their prayers for the sick and the dying is now completed. *Jewish Wisdom for Living and Dying* has been written for those who are sick and or dying and looking to the Jewish tradition for direction to help him or her face and deal with these life-threatening events. It has also been written for those who care for the sick, dying, or dead whether through *Bikur Holim* or *Chevra Kadisha* organizations. Finally, this book also was written for those who simply have an interest in these subjects and Jewish texts particularly from this period and location.

As interesting as this research and study has been, an important question needs to be asked: What do these two texts mean for the Jewish community of the 21st century? These texts were certainly exceedingly popular over the centuries, as evidenced by the numerous editions of both of them that have been published. Because they were both written for the *Chevra Kadisha*, the burial societies, in their communities and used by these societies to this very day, their prayers, rituals, and commentaries are most useful and interesting to the members of these societies.

Do these books also have a usefulness not only to burial societies but also to individuals who are either facing their own illnesses or their own deaths, or the illness and dying of family members, friends, and members of their communities? Do these books and their rituals offer a theological and psychological view of the sick and dying person, and his or her relationship to God, which can be helpful to a Jew today? Finally, if not literally, can the prayers and rituals described in these texts be adapted and even be rewritten for use by those facing illness and death?

The answer to these questions is yes, in that *Maavor Yabok* in particular is such a book that can be reworked and rewritten for a modern age. By its presentations of not only the rituals, but also the spiritual functioning of these rituals, that *Maavor Yabok* gives to the practitioners in the *Chevra Kadisha*, those who are ill, and those who are visiting the ill, not only a manual of what to do, but also a manual of how to do what needs to be done to be spiritually effective. This is what so many people going through these experiences look for and yearn for; a connection with the divine to give meaning, purpose to what the tradition asks of them to do and to say at these times during their lives.

Those who are ill, and particularly severely ill, quite often express their feelings of helplessness regarding his or her illness and treatment. Everything is being done to them and for them by the medical team or in the case of hospice, the care-giving team, but their question of what they can do for themselves spiritually is so often expressed and left unfulfilled. There are also the family members, friends, and members of the community who want to do something for their loved one and friend. However, either they do not know or do not have the resources to do more than be there with this person, who is in so much need spiritually at this difficult and trying time. When the doctor tells the patient and those who are supporting him or her that there is nothing more medically that can be done, they do not want to give up, at least spiritually. They wonder whether our tradition has any prayer or ritual that can help during this time of need.

People who have a more traditional background, in which they were taught many of the texts with their prayers and rituals shared in these books, know that they can always do something regarding illness and even facing death: There are prayers for healing. There are confessions of sin, the *Vidui*, before death. There are psalms that can be recited when all else is exhausted, and there is even a ritual called *Sh'nui Hashem*, the Changing of One's Name, to deceive the angel bringing on the illness or death, as to the spiritual identity of this patient. The Jewish tradition has an entire chest of spiritual tools to be offered at such a time. The challenge is to know where to find them and how to use them. This is where and when these texts, *Maavor Yabok* and *Sefer HaHayiim*, and others can come into play.

I can certainly recall the time when I, as a chaplain in a cancer center, was asked by the grandmother of a 14-year-old boy, who was lying in a coma with his lungs filled with over forty tumors, to recite psalms. During this tragic and desperate time for this family, she knew that when there seemed to be nothing medically to do, a person of the Jewish faith could turn to the beautiful psalms that function as a prayer to God for help. In response to her request, I went to the boy, held his hand, and recited psalms.

I also remember visiting another patient who was lying in her bed, breathing with much difficulty through the oxygen mask over her face. I approached her bed, sat beside it, took her hand, and introduced myself. Looking directly into my eyes, she asked me with great difficulty and in a whisper, "Rabbi, I cannot go through this anymore. Can you take my life? Please!"

My heart and soul were breaking for this woman, immediately seeing how tortured she was with each breath she tried to take. Looking at her, I said, "I would do this for you if I could, but I hope you understand that I can't." Knowing, however, the tradition and the sources as I do, I was able to comfort her soul by offering various prayers from the tradition such as the *Shema* and prayers for healing. I was familiar with the various spiritual tools the tradition offered that should be said as the end of life was drawing near. Her physical body wracked in pain, but she needed the spiritual outreach that only prayer and ritual held for the one who is suffering.

I said to her, "I am going to chant the Shema (Deuteronomy 6:4, "Hear O Israel, Adonai our God, Adonai is One," a prayer traditionally said before death). If you can chant these words with me, I welcome you to join me as best as you can." I began to chant the well-known words from the tradition. She joined with me in a whisper, in a "still small voice" (I Kings 19:11). As we chanted these words in a mantra-like fashion, I watched as her eyes slowly closed, and she fell off to sleep. At least for the moment, this spiritual tool from the closet of tools from our tradition brought her some comfort and ease. These tools are available if a person has been taught of them and knows to use them

I also recall the time when I was called into the preoperative waiting area to minister to a patient who cried out for spiritual help. She had just been given the answer by her surgeon to her question, "What are my odds going into this operation?" by his saying, "There is a 1% chance of your coming through alive." Having to face this surgery with these odds, she did not know what to do or what to say, but she had the need to turn to God. She asked for the Rabbi Chaplain to assist her in prayers to help her through this dire situation, since she did not know what to do or say. I received the call to go to her, and there in the pre-op area I was able to offer prayers from our tradition in both Hebrew and English giving her the strength to face what she needed to face. She did survive the operation.

These two texts, *Maavor Yabok* and *Sefer HaHayiim*, and their rituals, prayers, and explanations of these Jewish spiritual sources truly offer enormously powerful tools from the tradition for individuals. At these most vulnerable moments of life, a person can know that he or she can turn to their tradition for help. These rich sources have materials that allow the sick or dying person, or their loved ones and community, to know that even when medical professionals throw up their hands, there are still especially important and powerful words that can be offered and rituals that can be enacted. *Maavor Yabok* and *Sefer HaHayiim* offer access to spiritual tools that say to every person going through these challenging life situations and end of life events, "There is always something that we can do!"

Both books, in their attitudes toward sickness and death, their terminologies, and analyses, show the basic Judaic understanding of the process of sickness, dying, and death. For whether the liturgy's vocabulary is stated in terms of metaphysical concepts taken from the kabbalistic literature (i.e., a harmony or disharmony between the *Sefirot*, as expressed primarily in *Maavor Yabok*) or in more concrete theological terms of reward and punishment, as is found in the rabbinic literature and expressed primarily in *Sefer HaHayiim*, the liturgies and their commentaries and expositions define sickness and death in light of a person's sins. They then offer the sick and dying person the tools to confront these life's trials.

The difference between the texts is how each has the ill person or his or her visitors deal with sickness and dying and the tools to confront these life's experiences. In addition to the usual *Chevra Kadisha* ritual manual, *Maavor Yabok* offers a detailed description of how these various prayers and rituals function on a metaphysical level to bring about their desired effect upon the spiritual realms above, the divine, and the realm in which the sick and dying person and his community reside. This knowledge can give to the ill and dying hope that spiritual resources are available to him or her regardless of how desperate the situation might seem.

Moshe Idel described the benefit of the kabbalistic understanding of ritual and prayer when he wrote:

> A traditional type of religiosity, which is accretive par excellence, tends to reiterate earlier concepts, related to canonical texts and rituals, which are combined with new views in different ways.[1]

Maavor Yabok added this "new view" to the traditions for many prayers and rituals for the sick and dying. This addition to these traditional sources gave a new understanding of the processes of illness, dying, and death as well as a powerful metaphysical knowledge to affect the spiritual forces in operation at these times

---

1. Idel, *Primeval Evil*, LXI.

in a person's life. This understanding is helpful to the person who is sick or dying, but also is useful to the members of a *Chevra Kadisha* who yearn for ways to better understand the sacred rituals they perform and to add a spiritual depth to doing them.

I believe that an updated and rewritten *Maavor Yabok* could become a modern version of *The Tibetan Book of the Dead* for the Jewish community. It would offer a manual of what to do at the times of sickness, dying, and death, as well as an understanding of how these prayers and rituals have a cosmic effect upon the divine being. In this way, for someone using this text today, the same spiritual understanding and power can be used to confront these life experiences that happen to every person.

I have spoken to volunteers in *Chevra Kadisha* groups, particularly at conferences of an organization called, *Kavod v'Nichum*, and discovered that although these "workers" in this holy endeavor are fulfilling this important mitzvah, most are doing the rituals without an understanding of the spiritual underpinnings of their acts while visiting the sick, preparing the body, or during burial. They, however, do not know of or use the various *Kavanot,* or spiritual mindful intentions, that a kabbalistic knowledge of the function of these rituals brings to the fulfillment of these mitzvot. It is this author's belief that there is a need in the *Chevra Kadisha* community to take the rituals and the kabbalistic explanations and directions as given in *Maavor Yabok*, and to rewrite them in such a way that they can be used by modern practitioners as they perform these holy mitzvot.

The basic theme throughout both texts, as analyzed earlier, is that human actions, when fulfilling the mitzvot, and living a Torah life are seen in a positive light. When a person's actions fail to fulfill the mitzvot, they are seen in a negative light. The latter way leads to sin. The goal, then, of the person, sick or dying, lying in his or her bed in a hospital, hospice, or home, is to spend time evaluating his or her actions regarding those between the person and God, and the person and other people.

Such an evaluation must be followed with a true act of *Teshuvah*, that is repentance, which rebuilds the relationship with God that a person desires at these challenging times in life when quite often the feeling is one of abandonment. *Teshuvah* includes a *vidui*, or confession of misdeeds, and an attempt, if possible, to rectify hurts committed. *Tzedakah*, which is the giving of charity, is always seen to repair the sins that have been committed, especially when the specific sins cannot be addressed. This entire process, as described, is filled with prayers to God and the recitation of many verses from *Tanach* as ways to reach out to the Divine at such times in which the person feels so vulnerable and helpless.

All these themes can be reworded and reframed for people today and taught to those looking for a spiritual direction in their lives; a direction that is derived from these traditional sources and their viewpoints as to how to meet the spiritual needs of the moment.

The many verses from *Tanach* can be inspirational, but also instructive as to what actions need to be done at these times to confront one's sins and when possible, to redo the misdeeds. What *Maavor Yabok* does is to inform the sick or dying person, or the community of family and friends, that when all of these actions are conducted with proper kabbalistic intentions, directed by an educated understanding of the function of prayer and ritual upon the Divine being and therefore all of existence, the effect of the prayers, rituals, and readings is great indeed.

Both texts enable the sick or dying to overcome the often-felt experience expressed in the powerful words of Psalm 22, "My God, my God, why have you forsaken me?" and to believe as it says in Psalm 141, "God heals the brokenhearted." It is therefore important that the words and proscribed actions in both works, but particularly *Maavor Yabok*, need to be couched in such a way that they can be understood and used by those who are in need and who suffer physically, emotionally, and most importantly, spiritually today. These teachings can be so important to people today, when written in such a way that modern Jews can understand and use them. These rituals and prayers allow one to never feel alone and to never feel separated from the presence of God. I, therefore, see the need for a new *Maavor Yabok*.

I also see the need for a modernized text of *Maavor Yabok* to be used as a teaching tool for adult education programs and even in Hebrew Schools to children. The attitude expressed in these books and the traditional sources toward sickness, dying and death cannot be learned when a person is going through these life crises. These attitudes and the rituals' usage need to become a part of a person's life from his or her earliest years if they are to be most effective when needed later in life. Judaism does teach one how to die. This teaching must then be taught for the benefit of all, from the young to the old.

There is a reason *Maavor Yabok* is, in many respects, a Musar book teaching how to live life. One modern edition of *Maavor Yabok* has a subtitle on its cover, "How a person should conduct his life until his last day of life." [2] A person lives life to his or her fullest when he or she knows also how to die and accepts death as a part of life and the living of life. As Ascher wrote, "A truly religious and godly man will never suffer himself to be overtaken by death: he will always prepare for it . . ."[3] If this could be taught to the entire Jewish community, age appropriately of course, then these beautiful and meaningful rituals, prayers, and the understanding of them, could help one to live and to die, as well.

The actor Orson Welles is quoted as stoically declaring, "We're born alone, we live alone, we die alone." Although it is a fact that every person dies "alone", the existential feeling of aloneness is partly overcome when the rituals and prayers of these texts can be used and particularly when they are used in and by a caring community. The words embedded in these texts allow the sick and the dying person to reach out to the Infinite One, thereby overcoming the existential aloneness of illness and dying.

These prayers and rituals allow a person to believe that the answers to these prayers come not necessarily in the literal response to the words expressed in the prayers. The answers, rather, come from the knowledge and the existential experience that some spiritual being is there with a person, even as that last breath is

---

2. Berechiah, *Maavor Yabok*, Yedid HaSefarim

3. Ascher, *The Book of Life*, p. 125.

being taken, and thereby that person is not spiritually dying alone. What is most powerful is that this occurs while surrounded by a community of family and friends who are also grounded in these prayers and rituals and their spiritual underpinnings. All the rituals and prayers in both books are performed while surrounded by a community of family, friends, and or *Chevra Kadisha* members.

I walked into the room of a 19-year-old man who was dying of leukemia. The family surrounded his bed as I walked up to him, sat down, and took his hand. He opened his eyes, and his face was enmeshed in the oxygen mask that enabled him to continue breathing. I introduced myself as the hospital Rabbi coming by to say hello. His first words and only words to me that day were, "Rabbi, where is the justice in what is happening to me?" I responded, "I would be a fool to give you an answer!" A few minutes later, I left thus hospital room after letting his family know that I would return the next morning.

I did return, and Gary asked me to just hold his hands. I did for the next eight hours, sometimes talking and much of the time in silence, until he died. Gary's family asked me to officiate at his funeral. When I visited them during *Shiva*, the seven days of mourning after a Jewish burial, I asked them why Gary wanted me to hold his hands those hours before his death. They told me it was because of the honest answer I had given to his question.

Even decades later, I often recall this experience. My answer to Gary's question was really no answer at all, at least in terms of a verbalized answer. It was, however, an answer in a special and personal way. I was saying to him that, like Gary, I did not understand what was happening to him or why, but, along with his family, I would not leave him to die alone. We would not abandon him physically or spiritually. We would stay with him with love until the end, and beyond. I also would like to believe that by my answer, and that bond we experienced together, that the presence of God was felt by him, and that this was the answer to his question. That room of Gary's became the Gate of Heaven but until then we did now know this. (Genesis 28:17)

Reflections

Sacred books like *Maavor Yabok* and *Sefer HaHayiim* were written for members of the *Chevra Kadisha* as instruction manuals for their work. It is their work with the sick, the dying, the dead, and the mourners, as expressed through these books' rituals and prayers, that a community and God show that they will not abandon a person during these times of great physical, emotional, and spiritual distress. Judaism does offer the spiritual tools and weapons at these times to confront these experiences of life head-on. As the person reaches out to God and community with these tools and weapons, God, and community, in turn, reach out to him or her lying in that bed.

If once again modern man or woman can be taught in the ways of *Gemilut Hasadim*, "kindness and truth," the sick and dying will not live and die amidst sterility and loneliness, as so often happens, but rather experience these life's moments amidst a shared community. This will be a community of faith enveloped in the presence of God, bound together by caring, strength, and love in the face of the ultimate end of life, that is, death. By such texts such as *Maavor Yabok* and *Sefer HaHayiim*, people will then have the spiritual tools to deal with sickness, dying, and death in a positive and loving way. They will have the knowledge and ability to affect the journey of the soul as it moves on after death into the Infinite.

I challenge the *Chevra Kadisha* community to take on the task of writing a new manual for the 21st century which offers rituals and ceremonies for the sick, dying and dead sustained by a spiritual underpinning offered by the teachings of the Kabbalah heritage. How needed this is!

KABBALISTIC TERMS

Sefirah/Sefirot—"The light of God is unique and of equal force and quality. A *Sefirah* is in a way a "filter" which transforms this light in a particular force or attribute, by which the Creator guides the worlds."[1] There are 10 *Sefirot*: *Keter* (crown), *Hochmah* (wisdom), *Binah* (understanding), *Hesed* (kindness), *Gevurah* (restriction/judgement), *Tiferet* (balance/harmony), *Netzach* (unbounded physicality), *Hod* (restricted physicality), *Yesod* (self/introspection), *Malchut* (foundation/grounding).

Daat is a quasi *Sefirah* between *Hochmah* and *Binah* and is described as knowledge.

Kavanah is the concentration and intention that is brought to the prayers and rituals.

Yichud "is also the unification of names or letters, as to provoke a specific action or reaction . . . By concentrating on various permutations or letters or names of angels, one could make these superior forces act according to his will."[2]

---

1. Afilalo, *Kabbalah, Dictionary* p. 233.
2. Afilalo, p. 151.

Bibliography

Afilalo, Raphael. *Kabbalah Dictionary*, R. Raphael Kabbalah Editions, 2005.

Ascher, B. H., trans. *The Book of Life and the Expression of the Tongue*, London: B.H.Ascher, 1863.

Baer, G. *Tozeot Chaiim*. Rodelheim: Druck u. Verlag con I. Lehrberger und Comp., 1871.

Berechiah, Aaron b. Moses of Modena. *Maavor Yabok*: 1926; rpt. Bnai Berak: Yashfeh, 1927.

Caro, Joseph. *Shulhan Aruch*. 1565; rpt. New York., 1953.

Davidson, Israel. *Theasurus of Medieval Hebrew Poetry*. New York: Ktav Publ. House, Inc., 1970.

De Sola Pool, ed., and tran. *The Traditional Payer Book for Sabbath and Festivals*. New Hyde Park: University Books, Inc., 1960.

Frankfurter, Simon. *Sefer Hahayiim*. Amsterdam: Israel ben Avraham, 1717.

Friendlender, M., tran. *The Guide for the Perplexed*. New York: Dover, 1956.

Goldin, Hyman E. *Hamadrikh*. New York: Hebrew Publ. Co., 1956.

HaCohen, Aaron from Lunel. *Orchot Chajim*. Frienze, 1750.

Horowitz, Isaiah. *Shene Luhot Ha-Brit*. Jerusalem, 1923.

Hulme, William. *Dialogue in Despair*. Nashville: Abingdon Press, 1968.

Idel, Moshe. *Primeval Evil in Kabbalah*. Brooklyn: Ktav, p. LXI. Jastrow, Marcus. *A Dictionary*. New York: Pardes Publ. House., Inc., 1950.

Jewish Encyclopedia. New York: Funk & Wagnalls Co., 1912.

Kissane, Edward J. *The Book of Psalms*. Dublin: The Richview Press, 1953.

Kubler-Ross, Elizabeth. *On Death and Dying*. London: Collier-Macmillan, Ltd., 1972.

Lazaron, Morris S. *The Consolation of Our Faith*. Baltimore, 1928.

Lerner, David Leigh. "On Death and Dying – Jewishly." *Reconstructionist*. XL, No. 1, (1974), 11–15.

Linn, Louis, and Leo W. Schwartz. *Psychiatry and Religious Experience*. New York: Random House, 1958.

Marcus, Jacob R. *Communal Sick-Care in the German Ghetto*. Cinn.: The HUC Press, 1974.

Minor Tractates of the Talmud. London: Soncino Press, 1963.

Bibliography

Moore, George Foot. *Judaism*. Cambridge: Harvard University Press, 1966.

Pappenheim, M.S. *Ziduk Hadin*. Breslau, 1821.

Rehfuss. C. *Vollstandiges Andachts-Buch zum Gebrauche Bei Krankheitsfallen*. Frankfurt am Main: Dreuct un Verlag Undraeaifchen Buchhandlung, 1834.

Schechter, Solomon. *Aspects of Rabbinic Theology*. New York: Schochen Books, 1969.

Siegler, Miriam and Humphrey Osmond. "The 'Sick Role' Revisited." *The Hastings Center Studies*, 1, No. 3 (1973), 41–58.

Urbach, Ephraim E, *The Sages*. Jerusalem: Magnes Press, 1971.

Zangwill, Israel, tran. *Selected Religious Poems of Solomon Ibn Gabriol*. Phil: JPS. 1923.

BIBLIOGRAPHY OF HEBREW TEXTS

אוטולונגי, שמואל דוד בכ"ר יחיאל. קריאה נאמנה. וניצא, 1809

ברכיה, אהרון בן משה ממודינה. אשמורת הבוקר. מנטובה, 1614

מעבר יבק, ידיד הספרים, ירושלים. ברכיה, אהרון בן משה ממודינה

ברכיה, אהרון בן משה ממודינה. מעבור יבק. מנטוא, 1626

האלאס, נתן אליעזר. ארח כל אדם. בודאעעשט, 1902

לוריא, יצחק. שלחן ערוך של יצחק לוריא. ורשה, 1818

נחמן, משה בן. תורת האדם. ורשה, 1767

פראה, ברוך אברהם. ספר מעיל צדקה. מנטובא, 1767

פראקעל, רש"פ סג"ל. לוית המת. 1854

פרנקפורטה, שמעון. ספר החיים, 1717

קיצור מעבור יבק. דיענפורות, 1806

קיצור מעבור יבק. פרנגפורט עם ואדר, 1815

ראצניטץ, דוד. זכרון ליום אחרון. פראג, 1860

רפואת הנפש. אלטונא, 1809

רפואת נשמה, ווילהמסדורף, 1714